CW01<30440

WAR IN THE AIR II

THE AIR COMBAT PAINTINGS OF
MARK POSTLETHWAITE

VOLUME 2

DROGA DO NIEBA
Acrylic on linen, 48" x 20", 2011
In the collection of Nigel Szembel

WAR IN THE AIR II

THE AIR COMBAT PAINTINGS OF

MARK POSTLETHWAITE

VOLUME 2

Written by Mark Postlethwaite

WING LEADER

PUBLISHING

First published 2012.
Wing Leader
PO Box 223, Walton-on-Thames,
Surrey, KT12 3YQ
England
Tel. 0845 095 0346

All paintings © Mark Postlethwaite 2012
apart from the Osprey cover paintings which are
© Osprey Publishing 2012.

All Rights Reserved.
No part of this publication may be reproduced,
stored in any form of retrieval system, or
transmitted in any form or by any means without
prior permission in writing from the publishers.
The cutting and reselling of paintings from this
book is also strictly prohibited.

Design by Mark Postlethwaite GAvA

Printed by
Dimograf, Sp. Z o. o. Poland

Purchase this and other Red Kite books directly
from Red Kite's websites;

www.redkitebooks.co.uk
www.wingleader.co.uk

*A special limited edition of this book is available
with a bookplate bearing the original signatures
of several WWII veterans. For more details, please
see the websites or contact the publishers.*

Most of the paintings in this book are available to
purchase as limited edition prints and all images
are available for licensing for editorial use.
For more information please visit the artist's
website.
www.posart.com

Or contact him directly by email,
mark@posart.com

ISBN 978-1-908757-04-3

ITALIAN ACES OF WWI
Acrylic on board, 15" x 11", 2009
Private Collection, New Zealand

opposite page
303 SQUADRON
Acrylic on board, 22" x 12", 2009
In the Collection of Neil T Bremer

Contents

Mark Postlethwaite GAvA

Mark Postlethwaite is now established as one of the world's leading aviation artists. He is one of the very few in this field who can combine both an artistic appreciation and passion for flight alongside a sound technical and historical knowledge of the flying machines themselves. As such, his work is collected worldwide by Museums, Aerospace companies and private collectors who demand 100% accuracy in the historical and technical aspects of their paintings.

Born in Leicestershire, England in 1964, like many of his friends, Mark had only one ambition during his school years, and that was to fly fast jets with the RAF. At the age of 13 he was devastated to discover that his eyesight was less than perfect and therefore unsuitable for military flying. Eventually after leaving school at 16 and working for the Co-op for two years, Mark managed to get a job in photography, thanks mainly to a portfolio he had built up whilst working on a free local newspaper.

Photography soon became a good outlet for his inborn creativity and during his 10 years in the business he worked in most aspects of professional photography in London, Leicester and Nottingham, shooting everything from cat food to lingerie, *"I preferred the latter!"* he says.

Mark started to paint aircraft on canvas at the age of 17 as a hobby. A lifelong interest in flying and aviation history together with his professional knowledge of light through his career as a photographer, soon combined to produce work of the highest standards in this exacting field. In 1987, he became the first ever Artist in Residence at the Royal Air Force Museum, Hendon in what was the first major exhibition of his work.

At the age of 27, Mark was elected to become the youngest ever Full Member of the Guild of Aviation Artists and shortly after, left photography to make a full time profession in aviation art. His knowledge of his subject was put to the test only a month after when he competed in and won the TV quiz show The $64,000 Question answering questions on the Battle of Britain. His work so impressed the host Bob Monkhouse that he bought one of Mark's originals there and then.

Around this time, Mark was contacted by the Chairman of 30 Squadron Association RAF with a view to commissioning him to paint a 75th anniversary painting for the Squadron. He drove down to their base at RAF Lyneham and for the first time came into contact with the life that he had so wanted as a schoolboy. *"The first thing that struck me was why I hadn't considered joining the RAF in a different trade apart from flying"*, Mark reflects, *"It honestly just never crossed my mind at the time, it was either flying or nothing."*

The subsequent painting was received with great acclaim within the RAF and soon commissions were rolling in on a regular basis from various squadrons including a three year association with the world famous RAF Aerobatic Team The Red Arrows.

On top of this, and more importantly for Mark, the squadrons were offering him the chance to fly with them as part of the research process. By 1995, he had built up many hours of military flying in types such as the Hercules, VC10, Gazelle and Tucano in the UK, Germany and Cyprus. However, his boyhood ambition of flying in a fast jet still eluded him.

Then, on a grey autumn afternoon in 1996, Mark found himself sitting in a BAe Hawk of 208 Squadron at RAF Valley in North Wales ready for take off. An hour later after a thoroughly uncomfortable but exhilarating tail chase 20,000 ft above Snowdon, his feet touched the ground once more and he realised that his boyhood ambition had been finally achieved, in the most unexpected way possible. He flew again in a Hawk a few months later and then the following year

he topped all of this by spending an hour at low level in a Harrier, *"the most incredible experience of my life"* he reflects *"finished off with the famous Harrier bow, when the aircraft hovers above the ground and dips its nose towards the crowd."*

"As a boy I used to marvel at seeing the Harrier perform this trick at airshows, I never ever dreamed that one day I would be in the cockpit looking back"

In 2002 the first book of his paintings 'War in the Air' was published by The Crowood Press, providing Mark with another one of those lifetime ambitions fulfilled. This second volume, being launched at the RAF Museum Hendon on the 25th Anniversary of his Artist in Residence there, fulfils another.

In 2004 Mark was approached by Osprey to take over from Ian Wyllie to paint all of their aviation book covers. Since then he has completed over 100 covers in three major and very popular series, thus ensuring that his work is seen in bookshops around the world.

He is basically self taught, and developed a style, when younger, based on his favourite artists of the time Frank Wootton, Michael Turner and the Airfix box art genius Roy Cross. Over the years his work has developed its own style and is now as recognisable as that of his boyhood idols.

He works exclusively in acrylic on canvas and board and is probably one of UK's foremost exponents of this modern paint. An easy medium to learn but a very difficult medium to master, Mark's acrylic paintings are nearly always mistaken for oil paintings due to the richness and thickness of paint he uses.

"Although there are many and varied reasons for using acrylics rather than oils, the principal benefit is that within minutes of finishing the painting the paint is completely dry". *"As most of my professional work has very tight deadlines, especially the book covers, I know that with acrylics I can scan them within minutes of completing the finishing touches."* *"This is just impossible with oils"*.

The principal element in all of Mark's work is the handling of light. Having spent 10 years in photography, he developed an enormous appreciation of the positioning, colouring and diffusion of light sources. This is clearly evident in his paintings.

"I love studying light and its associated tricks and nuances. As a photographer, when you have to make a plate of cat food look interesting, you realise that the only answer lies in the lighting! You soon learn that you can add colour, texture and mood all through the careful manipulation of light. When it comes to painting, the same rules apply and, historical accuracy permitting, the artist should use every trick he can to suggest the mood of the moment."

The biggest factor for which Mark's work is known around the world is his attention to historical accuracy. Having studied aviation all of his life and written several books on the subject, he knows his subject and never uses 'artistic licence' when painting historical scenes, *" I just think that it's disrespectful to the airmen we paint if we don't strive to capture the moment exactly as it appeared when it took place. Sometimes this can make the painting far more difficult, especially with regard to weather conditions and markings, but I just don't see the point in painting a 'nearly accurate' painting!"*

Mark married his Polish wife Asia in 1997 after a chance meeting on a train 2 years previously. The couple now have two children, Kasia (12) and Szymek (5) and live in Wrocław in south west Poland. They still have a house in England and Mark spends his time equally between the two countries. In his spare time, Mark is co-founder of Red Kite, www.redkitebooks.co.uk , a successful aviation book publishing company and still runs a WWII photo library, www.ww2images.com which now has over 15,000 photos online, all of which have been captioned by Mark himself!

Immediately after landing following a flight in the glorious FE2b at Masterton, New Zealand, I suddenly feel brave enough to stand again!

So here it is, the artist's equivalent of that difficult second album. You put your life's work into your first book and then 18 months later, your publishers demand another one, even though you're still in re-hab from the stress of producing the first one. Well, fortunately for me, there was no publisher demanding another book, (I had decided very early on to publish the next one myself), and I'm the world's most laid back commissioning editor, having now allowed myself eight long years before finally getting round to Volume II. This long gap has at least enabled me to build a much larger selection of work to choose from than I had for Volume 1 and as such I've decided to reduce the amount of historical text and photos and replace them with extra paintings, giving us a total of 100 throughout the book. Many of the paintings in this book are taken from the large collection that I've completed for Osprey Publishing over the last 8 years. These small 15" x 11" paintings are a pleasure to paint as they give me the opportunity to tackle subjects that would not be commercially viable in any other way. Subjects ranging from Fokker EIIIs right up to the B-2 Stealth Bomber have been covered over the years and I've included a selection of them here, to add a much needed bit of variety.

I wrote the introduction to Volume One from a hotel within the Arctic Circle near Narvik and pondered on the marvellously random life a professional artist leads, not knowing where his next commission might come from or indeed take him to. I presumed that it couldn't really

get any better than touring northern Norway on a research trip and sitting on a mountain at 3am watching the midnight sun kiss the tops of the distant islands. Yet in February 2010, my perceptions were changed when my wife and I found ourselves on a misty Dubai morning, boarding a huge Airbus A380 bound for Auckland on the other side of the world.

It had been not long after my first book was published that I received an email one morning from a very nice chap called Peter who wanted to buy a few of my WWI originals, a few Lancaster prints and maybe talk about a commission or two. I told my wife Asia the good news and replied to him offering a nice discount for such a generous order and started to prepare the paintings. Being a bit slow on the uptake, it took me a few days to eventually realise that this nice bloke called Peter was actually one of the most famous film directors in the world, Peter Jackson. (Now Sir Peter). His passion for WWI aviation was well known and there were rumours at the time about his interest in the remaking of the classic film 'The Dambusters' hence his interest in Lancaster prints. I quickly apologised for being slow to realise what his day job was and over the following years he became a much valued patron of my work. On a few occasions he mentioned that if I was ever passing his way I should pop

Above and below left; Flying alongside classic aircraft such as the SE5a above and Pfalz below left, really gives an aviation artist a new perspective on the human side of air combat. The pilots in these open cockpit aircraft are very visible to each other and it is not difficult to understand why there was maybe a greater sense of chivalry between them than in any subsequent air war.

in to Masterton and go and fly in his rapidly growing collection of WWI aircraft. Being that 'his way' was on the other side of the world in New Zealand I figured it was the email equivalent of saying you must meet up with people you'd shared a Sangria with in Torremolinos one evening, polite but never likely to happen!

However, with the ominous approach of my wife's 40th birthday and no idea whatsoever of a suitable present I was beginning to consider desperate measures, especially as she had been school champion in both grenade throwing and pistol shooting...(the benefit of a Communist Bloc education)... A germ of an idea started to form... how about a once in a lifetime trip to somewhere exotic... New Zealand for example. I quietly emailed Sir Peter to check if the offer of flying still stood, to which he generously replied yes, and so I proposed the idea to my grenade wielding better half. Luckily enough she quite liked the idea!

After a frenzy of ticket booking and children sorting we left the frozen snow-covered fields of Poland and within a few days were basking on the hot Pacific beaches on New Zealand's northern coast, not quite believing what we were doing. A few days later we drove down to

I quietly ask Sir Peter Jackson if he has any live grenades on show in the office as my wife Asia appears to have something behind her back...

Wellington and prepared for a day's flying at Masterton where the chief pilot and equally nice bloke, Gene De Marco opened the hangar and casually enquired as to which ones I fancied having a go in. Sensibly sticking to the two seaters for safety reasons I elected for the BE2f and the FE2b. On both sorties, they arranged for an SE5a and then a Pfalz to fly alongside my aircraft, just to 'make it more interesting'! I have been fortunate in my career to fly in many military aircraft, fast jets, helicopters etc but I never imagined in my wildest dreams that I would one day be crouching in the seatless gunner's compartment of an FE2b, holding on bravely to anything that looked solid as assorted airborne bugs flew backwards towards me at 90mph. The permanent grin I had on my face meant that I had to scrape some of the said bugs off my teeth afterwards, but it was worth it.

The day before we were due to fly home, we met with Gene and Sir Peter at the TVAL workshops in Wellington where they gave us a guided tour of the various projects in hand, including the vast array of aircraft and equipment already assembled for the Dambuster film. For 5 bizarre minutes I found myself sitting in the pilot's seat of a genuine Lancaster forward fuselage, with Sir Peter Jackson in the Flight Engineer's position drinking tea and my wife navigating. It only need Gollum to shout 'bombs away' from down in the nose and my seriously weird acid trip would have been complete, and I'd only had a chocolate biscuit...

The Lancaster has always been my favourite aircraft and over the years I have spent many hours researching its exploits with RAF Bomber Command, especially concerning the Dambuster Raid. I was very excited therefore, shortly after returning from New Zealand, when my publishing partner Simon Parry casually mentioned the fact that he had not only located the crash site of one of the Dams Raid Lancs, but also that he planned to go and recover it. The project soon snowballed as we spread the word, with many TV channels expressing an interest in covering the excavation. In the end, Cy Chadwick and ATypical Media came along to make a documentary entitled 'Last of the Dambusters' for Channel 5 and the History Channel.

We assembled in a cold, damp cow field just outside Doullens in France to assess the location, having already done a couple of surveys earlier in the year. Very soon we were uncovering small pieces of wreckage which proved that we were indeed on the last resting place of ED825, Joe McCarthy's Dambuster Lanc, which had crashed a few months after the Dams Raid on a Special Operations mission. After a full day's digging we unearthed a strange wooden framed object which we could only assume was a supply canister that would have been dropped to the Resistance fighters. We pondered on its identity overnight and the following morning extracted it from the ground for a closer inspection. Luckily we had the world's leading expert on the Type 464 there, Alex Bateman who suddenly had a flash of inspiration. Dashing back to the car, he returned with a large set of blueprints and the news that we had just found the under-gun position which was without doubt the rarest thing we could possibly have found! Not even all Type 464s had this gun mounting as it was found to be totally useless for the operation.

Standing in a cold and damp cow field near Doullens, Alex Bateman and I try to work out the identity of the mystery piece of wreckage from ED825. It turned out to be the rare undergun mount / escape hatch which must have been jettisoned just before the crash. Half an hour later, I carefully scraped the mud off a heavy lump of metal which turned out to be a hand grenade from the supply canister! My first instinctive thought was to swap it to my right, non-painting hand, my next thought was, 'where did everybody go'?? Luckily it was pretty intact and stable but I decided not to take it home as I'm sure Asia would have used it on me during our next 'family disagreement'! (photo. Brian Fernley)

Later in the day, Joe McCarthy's bomb-aimer George 'Johnny' Johnson arrived to see how we had got on and to do a piece to camera. Within minutes, it was clear that the carefully planned documentary about a few muddy blokes and the recovery of a Lancaster was now going to be a documentary about Johnny and his return to the continent. Johnny quite simply stole the show and we all stood enthralled as he talked us through the Dams raid on the dark hillside with the aid of a model Lanc and a model dam that we'd created earlier in the day.

The final result was a truly moving documentary with Johnny standing for the first time on the Sorpe Dam which he had tried so hard to destroy some 65 years before.

Moments and experiences such as these are what makes being an aviation artist so special; and they all came about because one day I decided I wanted to paint aircraft for a living. It may not attract the adulation of teenage girls or bring me untold riches like being in a band would, but then again, I reckon I'm far too old for all that nonsense now...

MP. Wrocław June 2012

A (Quixotic) Work in Progress - Veterans

*O*ver the past 20 years, I've been extremely lucky to have met and chatted to many ex-Bomber Command aircrew. I've always been fascinated by them as they were just ordinary young men who volunteered to do their bit for the war effort. Most of them agreed that the worst part of any operation was the hour before take-off when they were bused out to their distant dispersal ready to board their aircraft. For many of them it was hard to keep their nerves under control, knowing that this might be the night that they would die a violent and horrible death, or be badly injured by flak or fighters. Strangely enough, once on-board, for many the nerves disappeared as they went about their duties and concentrated on getting the bomber to their objective.

It was this final walk to the aircraft therefore that I wanted to capture in Veterans. The scene was so strong in my head that I didn't work on any preliminary sketches, (never a good idea!), I just went straight in and applied paint to canvas.

My main concept was to have the Lancaster very dark and towering over the men, with a bleak and cold wintry landscape all around. We would be walking with the men and none of them should be talking to each other, each one lost in his own thoughts.

In the first picture here, I have applied a loose grey cloudbase to the sky and roughly blocked in the Lancaster and snow. I've worked on the background trees and started to think about the shape of the dispersal pan and reflections in the concrete. This is probably as close as I'll get to my original bleak concept with a very monochrome palette and no strong direct light. I love grey, in fact grey is my favourite colour, as within it you can have all the colours of the rainbow. But it's also the hardest colour to use successfully and although many of my paintings start off all grey and moody, most of them end up colourful and 'optimistic'... which is really annoying!

In picture 2, I've added another coat of paint to the aircraft, played with the reflections on the perspex and worked on the background landscape. You'll also notice a stronger yellow clearing to the horizon. The horizon is so important in a painting as it gives the artist the ultimate extent of depth in his painting. However, with this painting I was constantly torn between having a distant clear horizon, for depth, or a dark foreboding cloud for atmosphere. You'll see it alternates several times during the course of the painting...

Picture 3 is quite a bit further on. You can see the horizon has reverted back to dark grey, the foreground snow has increased and the trees in the background have changed significantly as I tried to work out whether we needed depth on the left of the picture. It's often the case that you create by accident a really nice small section which you desperately try to preserve. Unfortunately it's also often the case that in the end you have to remove it to make the picture work as a whole. This happened with the trees on the left in the first two pictures, which I really liked. Unfortunately I felt that the painting needed a stronger vertical there so I added the Elm tree and enlarged the background trees.

I also added some figures for the first time as I needed to get a feel for where they might be. I was toying with the idea of just having six men as the viewer could then feel like the seventh. However, I could just imagine the letters I'd get from enthusiasts pointing out that the Lancaster had a crew of seven, so I decided to add an extra man, to save postage...

In picture 4, the painting now has its seventh sky, and again a clearance has appeared in the distance. I've also done a bit of de-forestation on the left to give us some depth through the tailplane. I've lost two of the men in the process, I can't remember how many times I lost the propellers as the new skies came and went!

I really loved the yellow sun reflected in the bomb aimer's blister and was desperate to keep it. I think my only problem at this point was that it looked a bit mid-dayish and not late evening.

Picture 5 has probably my favourite sky of all of them and I sometimes wish I just finished it up from here. The dark horizon has a lovely threatening feel to it and there is still a nicely limited palette to the whole picture. I've reintroduced the two men further away with the seventh man climbing aboard. I've also extended the concrete out of the picture to the right, giving us a lead into the picture and a nice area of grey to reflect the sky. There's also more snow in the foreground, as the picture becomes ever more busy this was one area that could provide a simplified balance. You can also see for the first time, a lot of detail added to the Lancaster, especially the cockpit and engines.

By picture 6 I was getting pretty frustrated with the whole thing as the sky had got the clearance again and colour was creeping in. I think the reason I did it was to make it more like late evening so I moved the light source round to more behind the aircraft and added some colour and texture to the clouds above the left-hand trees, which you'll notice have been trimmed quite a bit. I've also cleared some of the snow from behind the aircraft as this area has a critical effect on how far it appears away from the tail section.

Picture 7 at last starts to show a final stages sort of feel as detail gets added to the foreground and a Lancaster appears in the distance. The most significant addition here is the blue sky clearing to the right of the picture. This was totally against my original concept but I felt it was needed to cool the picture down and balance the warmth of the sunset. The trees have grown again on the left hand side, despite me really liking the cloud that was there... I just felt that the composition needed a stronger support in this area.

The last picture is of the final result which you can also see on page 108. A mass of small details have been added such as the mascot in the nearest airman's boot, the Trolley Acc and a few more footprints.

I should probably subtitle this section 'How not to paint a picture' as the lack of planning wasted so much time as I struggled with achieving my vision. However, the sheer excitement of just playing with the paint and trying to capture the atmosphere is worth the frustration even when it doesn't quite work. I live in hope, like most quixotic artists, that one day it will...

World War I

Early German Aces of WWI

Ltn d R Max Immelmann shoots down the 11 Squadron Vickers FB 5 Gunbus of Captain C C Darley on 26th October 1915 near Arras. This was Immelmann's fifth aerial victory making him one of the world's first air aces. He was killed in action on 18th June 1916.

Max Immelmann

EARLY GERMAN ACES OF WWI
Acrylic on board, 15" x 11", 2007
Private collection, New Zealand

Pusher Aces
of WWI

On 22nd November 1916 a flight of five Albatros DIIs of Jasta Boelcke were flying west of Bapaume when they were bounced by RFC fighters. In the ensuing dogfight Jasta Boelcke's commanding officer Oblt Stefan Kirmaier was hit by the guns of Captain John Andrews flying a 24 Squadron DH 2 and crashed on the British side of the front line. He had been killed by a single bullet in the head.

This loss, coming soon after the loss of the legendary Boelcke himself, was a bitter blow for the Jasta. But the following day Jasta Boelcke gained revenge of some sort when one of its young pilots, Ltn Manfred von Richthofen, shot down and killed the famous British pilot Major Lanoe Hawker VC, the C/O of 24 Squadron*.

(*See next page)

PUSHER ACES OF WWI
Acrylic on board, 15" x 11", 2009
Private collection, New Zealand

THE DEATH OF HAWKER VC
Acrylic on board, 20" x 14", 2011
Private collection, New Zealand

The Death of Hawker VC

Ltn Manfred von Richthofen dives on DH 2s of 24 Squadron on 23rd November 1916. After a brief combat, the lead DH 2 flown by Major Lanoe Hawker VC was seen in a turning fight with the dark brown Albatros DII of von Richthofen. The two aces turned and turned, producing a deadly stalemate until, running short of fuel, Hawker broke off and headed for the British lines. In one of von Richthofen's parting shots, Hawker was hit in the head and killed instantly, his aircraft falling just south of Bapaume. Kirmaier had been avenged.

Balloon Busting Aces of WWI

On 15th May 1918, Adjutant Willy Coppens of the 9ème Escadrille Aviation Militaire Belge attacked a German balloon over the Houthulst Forest. Just as he was flying over the damaged balloon, it lurched upwards and collided with his Hanriot HD 1. Thinking quickly, he switched the engine off and waited as the biplane slid off the side of the balloon. Heading rapidly towards the ground, he restarted the engine and survived to claim a Belgian record total of 35 balloons destroyed.

BALLOON BUSTING ACES OF WWI
Acrylic on board, 15" x 11", 2006
Private collection, New Zealand

Facing the Enemy

FE2bs of 25 Squadron engage Fokker E IIIs near Lille during the spring of 1916. This was air fighting in its infancy with both aircraft being designed as fighters. The Fokker was advanced in that it had a machine gun that fired through the propeller arc enabling the pilot to steer his aircraft into a natural firing position behind his prey. The 'Fee' on the other hand, placed the propeller behind the pilot and gave him a gunner at the front to worry about the shooting part. This extra weight meant that the FE2b was large, cumbersome and pretty slow, none of which are qualities suited to a fighter aircraft. Within a year both aircraft would be obsolete as far more modern and manoeuvrable fighters were introduced on both sides.

I was lucky enough to fly in Sir Peter Jackson's FE2b back in 2010 at Masterton, New Zealand and after landing, I knew I had to paint this wonderful aircraft. Having just spent half an hour in the gunner's position holding on bravely to the floor... I also knew the focus had to be on the poor gunner who didn't even have the comfort of a seat and was always in danger of falling out. The common adversary at the time would have been the new Fokker E III so I placed them together, with the Fokker pilots having made an unwise head-on pass. The one thing you notice during formation flying is how visible the pilot is, especially in open cockpit aircraft such as these. I therefore had the Fokker pilot and the Fee gunner exchanging glances as they passed each other by, not knowing like us, who would end up the victor in this encounter.

Chief pilot Gene De Marco gives me the pre-flight safety demonstration on the FE2b, basically 'attach this wire to your harness and hang on tight...!'

FACING THE ENEMY
Acrylic on linen, 48" x 24", 2010
Private Collection, New Zealand.

60 SQUADRON
Acrylic on board, 15" x 11", 2011
Private collection, New Zealand

60 Squadron

On 19th May 1917, a lone green and yellow Albatros inadvertently popped out of cloud directly over the aerodrome where 60 Squadron's C Flight was about to take off in its Nieuport scouts. Scurrying quickly back into the cloud, Ltn Georg Noth made for the German lines but was soon caught and forced down by the Nieuport (B1602) of William Fry. Noth was taken prisoner and his colourful Albatros was sent to the UK for evaluation.

Bristol F 2 Fighter Aces of WWI

On 13th March 1918, Bristol F 2 Fighters of 62 Squadron clashed with assorted German fighters near Cambrai. In the ensuing dogfight, the 'Red Baron's' younger brother Lothar von Richthofen was wounded when his red and yellow Fokker Dr I was hit by the gunner of one of the Bristol fighters.

BRISTOL F 2 FIGHTER ACES OF WWI
Acrylic on board, 15" x 11", 2007
Private collection, New Zealand

Austro-Hungarian Aces of WWI

An Austro-Hungarian Albatros DIII flown by Brumowski forces down an Italian Macchi L.3 4842, near Baseleghe, northern Italy on 5th November 1917.

Both of these paintings use a similar viewpoint on the main aircraft which I find works very well for biplanes. The strong converging perspective of the upper and lower wings draws your eye into the picture and up towards the unfortunate secondary aircraft, which is usually in the process of being shot down. The only drawback of this viewpoint is that the wheels need to be very well painted with perfect ellipses, and I hate doing wheels, that's why I never paint trains!

Spad XIII
v
Fokker DVII

On 26th September 1918, Vzfw Karl Weinmann of Jasta 50 was attacking an Allied balloon when he was bounced by Spads. Sous-Lt René Schurck, Adj Emile Régnier and the C/O of SPA12, Capt Armand de Turenne all fired at the unfortunate Fokker, seen here trailing smoke. Turenne's aircraft in the foreground is still wearing the cockerel's head of his previous unit SPA48.

AUSTRO-HUNGARIAN ACES OF WWI
Acrylic on board, 15" x 11", 2012
Private collection, New Zealand

SPAD XIII V FOKKER DVII
Acrylic on board, 20" x 14", 2008
Private collection, New Zealand

23

The First of Many

Oblt z S Friedrich Christiansen in his Hansa-Brandenburg W12 floatplane from Zeebrugge naval station shoots down a Felixstowe-based Curtiss H12B Large America flying boat on 15th February 1918. Its Canadian crew included one American, Alfred Dillon Sturtevant, an officer of the US Naval Reserve attached to RNAS Felixstowe since October 1917. He became the first American of any military branch to die in aerial combat in his own country's service during World War 1.

THE FIRST OF MANY
Acrylic on board, 15" x 11", 2011
Private collection, New Zealand

GOTHAS OVER LONDON
Acrylic on canvas, 42" x 28", 2006
Private collection, New Zealand

On 13th June 1917 a large force of Gotha bombers carried out a daylight bombing raid on London for the first time. Over 160 people died as a result providing a terrible forewarning of what was to come in the Second World War for not only London, but also Guernica, Warsaw, Hamburg and ultimately, Hiroshima.

Gothas over London

SE 5/5a Aces of WWI

Lieutenant George J Cox of 2 Squadron, Australian Flying Corps, dives through a formation of enemy aircraft, claiming one Fokker DVII with an accurate burst of fire, 27th August 1918. Cox followed this up with a further victory a few minutes later, making him an Ace. However, a month later his luck ran out when his aircraft was hit over enemy lines and he was taken prisoner.

McCudden in Combat

On the morning of 30th January 1918, legendary Ace Captain James McCudden of 56 Squadron took off alone to go on one of his usual high altitude patrols. He came across five enemy aircraft some 4000ft below him and swooped into attack, quickly claiming two destroyed and generally panicking the remaining three. McCudden's SE5 was unusual in that it was fitted with a captured German spinner, painted bright red. By the time of his death in a flying accident in July 1918, McCudden had shot down 57 enemy aircraft and had been awarded the Victoria Cross. He was just 23 years old.

SE5/5a ACES OF WWI
Acrylic on board, 5" x 11", 2007
Private collection, New Zealand

McCUDDEN IN COMBAT
Acrylic on board, 15" x 11", 2009
Private collection, New Zealand

Jasta 18
The Red Noses

On the morning of 12th August 1918, Ltn d R Kurt Monnington was flying with Jasta 18 high over southwest Germany on patrol At about 12,000 feet over Schirmeck, the pilots of Staffel Raben sighted two formations of DH 9s of 104 Squadron. Monnington closed in on one of the bombers in the trailing group and opened up. The fuel tanks of DH 9 D2931 were hit and its pilot 2Lt O F Meyer was doused in petrol. Monnington watched as the RAF pilot struggled to land the crippled aircraft before it could burst into flames; Meyer landed it intact on Bühl aerodrome where he and observer Sgt Wallace were taken prisoner.

JASTA 18 - THE RED NOSES
Acrylic on board, 15" x 11", 2010
Private collection, New Zealand

ACES HIGH
Acrylic on board, 15" x 11", 2009
Private collection, New Zealand

On 29th July 1917, three colourful SE 5s of 60 Squadron were bounced by Albatros DVs of Jasta 12. Two of the 60 Squadron pilots were experienced Aces, Captain 'Billy' Bishop and Captain 'Grid' Caldwell and successfully fought their way out of trouble, but the third pilot, 2Lt Gunner was not so lucky, becoming Jasta 12's 100th aerial victory. The colourful SE 5 markings were flight colours, red for A Flight, yellow for B Flight and blue for C Flight, but were soon replaced by less exotic markings, leaving the Germans to bring colour to the skies over France for the rest of the war.

Aces High

Republican Aces of the Spanish Civil War

Sergeant Garcia La Calle's Hawker Fury in action against Nationalist Fiat CR-32s over Toledo on 31st August 1936 during the Spanish Civil War. The Hawker Fury was the last of Hawker's biplane fighters, and probably the most elegant.

FIAT CR-32 ACES
Acrylic on board, 15" x 11", 2010
In the collection of Egidio Gavazzi

REPUBLICAN ACES OF THE SPANISH CIVIL WAR
Acrylic on board, 15" x 11", 2011
Artist's collection

Aces of the Legion Condor

Leutnant Rudolf Goy of 3.J/88 scored three victories in Spain and went on to fly with II./JG 53. This painting shows Goy in action in his Messerschmitt Bf109D on the 19th July 1938 during the Nationalist offensive towards the Mediterranean, between Segorbe and Viver, just east of Valencia, south-eastern Spain.

OK so here's a little secret. When working on these Osprey covers, time is usually tight and certainly too tight for me to make a model of the background aircraft. As such, when I need a quick angle on an aircraft such as the I-16 Rata pictured here and on the opposite page in the CR-32 Aces cover art, I tend to dig out my old favourite photos and work from them. If you study the two Ratas in these two paintings, you'll notice that the angle is exactly the same, as it's taken from the same photo source. Now that you know the secret, look out for an Albatros DV that has been shot down in at least three of my Osprey covers, although I'm thankful to say only one of them appears in this book!

ACES OF THE LEGION CONDOR
Acrylic on board, 15" x 11", 2010
Artist's collection

MARK POSTLETHWAITE '11

World War II

RUNNING OUT OF OPTIONS
Acrylic on canvas, 16" x 12", 2010
In the collection of David Layne

Running out of Options

A Hampden crew of 50 Squadron search in vain for their home airfield at Waddington in the low lying early morning mist. With their fuel about to run out, they eventually managed to put the aircraft down in a field not far from the airfield.

Daylight over Brest

Sgt Peter McDermott and his 144 Squadron Hampden crew battle through fierce flak over Brest, 24th December 1941. They were sent on a near suicide mission to bomb the Scharnhorst and Gneisenau in broad daylight over one of the most heavily defended ports in Europe. Despite being extensively damaged, they managed to get home.

Wing Commander Peter McDermott told me the incredible story of this raid when I was writing my book Hampden Squadrons in Focus. A few years later, Nick Stroud at Aeroplane magazine asked me if I knew any good Hampden stories for a piece of cover art and I instantly thought of this one. I went ahead and produced the painting opposite and sent a scan to the magazine and a print to Wg Cdr McDermott for his approval. The following day I received a phone call to say that Peter had died the day before my letter arrived.

DAYLIGHT OVER BREST
Acrylic on board, 20" x 12", 2009
In the collection of Dave Robinson

Oslo Defenders

Gladiators of the Norwegian Army Air Force engage Messerschmitt Bf110s of ZG76 south of Oslo, early on the morning of 9th April 1940. Sersjant Schye flying Gladiator 427 managed to bring down the Bf110 of Uffz. Mutschele before being shot down himself moments later. Schye put his smoking Gladiator down onto a frozen lake but ended up overshooting into a nearby field. He escaped with minor injuries. In the background, Heinkel He111s head north to bomb targets in the Oslo area.

In preparation for this painting I read all the available accounts of the Norwegian pilots who went up on this momentous morning to face the German onslaught. I had already painted the sinking of the Blücher which took place a few hours before so I had a good feel for the weather conditions on the day.

I then prepared these three sketches for the Norwegian clients to consider. I preferred the rear view of the Gladiator as it showed the Norwegian colours on the rudder and upper wings. In the end I think I preferred sketch A as it had a bit more movement in it but the client leant towards sketch C. As you can see, the final result ended up being a bit of both!

OSLO DEFENDERS
Acrylic on linen, 42" x 24", 2006
In the collection of The Norwegian Armed Forces

MARK POSTLETHWAITE GAvA '06

SURPRISE ATTACK
Acrylic on linen, 42" x 24", 2007
In the collection of The Norwegian Armed Forces

Surprise Attack

At the end of May 1940, the German invasion of Norway was reaching ever further north. Hurricanes of 46 Squadron had been hurriedly shipped north and were now based at Bardufoss, north of Narvik. On the afternoon of 28th May, three Hurricanes led by the New Zealander Flight Lieutenant Pat Jameson were on a routine patrol just north of Narvik when they spotted two German seaplanes hidden deep in Rombaksfjord. The seaplanes, both rare Dornier 26s, had just landed to offload German mountain troops and arms into the area and were now totally vulnerable to attack. 'Seeadler' (P5+AH WNr.0791) and 'Seemöwe' (P5+CH WNr.0793), were attacked repeatedly and both aircraft were sunk in situ.

Just two weeks later, this tranquil fjord again echoed to the sound of war as during the second Battle of Narvik, the German destroyer Georg Thiele ran aground just behind the far Do26's port wingtip.

I've been painting Norwegian history for nearly 20 years now and this was one combat I had always wanted to do. The Dornier 26 was such a rare but good looking aircraft and to be able to paint it in a spectacular Norwegian fjord was just too good an opportunity to miss!

I took my wife and 5 year old daughter up to Narvik for the research trip and with the help of a Norwegian friend we trekked along the steep wooded side of Rombaksfjord until we came to the wreck of the Georg Thiele. It was a spectacular sight and remarkable in that it lay only a few hundred meters from the last resting place of the two Do26s. I took plenty of reference photos whilst Kasia threw stones into the water around the wreck. (A few years afterwards, the wreck crashed back down into the water and we have convinced Kasia that it was her stones that did it!) We then trekked back and visited the Narvik War Museum where pieces of Seeadler are on display. It's well worth a visit if you're ever in the area.

Taking off from Bardufoss on the way home, we flew over Narvik and as you can imagine, although my body was sitting in a comfortable MD83, my imagination was at the controls of a Hurricane looking out for enemy aircraft!

Below; My wife Asia and daughter Kasia next to the George Thiele in 2004. The painting's viewpoint is located from approximately where the yellow cross is looking back towards the camera. Kasia appears to have just realised that we've got to walk another 2hrs back in the opposite direction!

MARK POSTLETHWAITE GAvA '07

FIRST VICTORY
Acrylic on linen, 3¼" x 18", 2011
In the collection of Richard Kornicki

First Victory

On 30th August 1940, pilots of 303 (Polish) Squadron were on a routine training sortie, still frustratedly kicking their heels and waiting for Fighter Command to allow them to enter the Battle of Britain, when one of the pilots spotted a formation of enemy bombers. Without hesitating he broke away to intercept, despite orders to stay in formation. The pilot, Ludwik Paszkiewicz engaged and shot down a Messerschmitt Bf110 thus scoring the squadron's first ever aerial victory in the Battle of Britain. He was later admonished by the C/O for disobeying orders before then being congratulated by him for proving to Fighter Command that the squadron was ready for operational flying!

This event provided the inspiration for a similar story in the classic 1969 film 'Battle of Britain'.

The painting depicts Paszkiewicz in Hurricane RF-V R4217, shooting down the Bf110 M8+MM of 4/ZG76 near Kimpton in Hertfordshire. In the background, a Hurricane of 56 Squadron flown by P/O B J Wicks closes in to also have a go at the doomed German fighter. High up to the top left of the picture, the rest of 303 Squadron continue with their training mission.

Having married a Pole some 15 years ago, I've long felt a need to paint more Polish subjects and this particular combat stands out as one of the most significant in Polish aviation history.

The opportunity to paint it came about when I was asked to put my Droga do Nieba painting* into a fund-raising auction at the RAF Museum, Hendon. As it was a Polish themed night I decided to paint this scene as well to go alongside the larger painting. That night I was very pleased to see both paintings go to households with very strong and proud Polish roots, in fact I understand that this painting is now on loan to the museum at RAF Northolt from where 303 Squadron fought their Battle of Britain.

* see page 46

Combat over Croydon

On 15th August 1940, Messerschmitt Bf110s of Epr. Gr. 210 took off in the early evening for a precision hit and run raid against the RAF Sector station at Kenley. As they flew towards the glare of the low evening sun, the leader and Gruppenkommandeur Walter Rubensdörffer mis-identified nearby Croydon aerodrome as the target and launched a devastating attack on the buildings and factories around the perimeter. As the Bf110s climbed off target they were intercepted by Hurricanes of 111 Squadron and 32 Squadron and an intense aerial combat took place, with the Hurricanes harrying the Bf110's all the way back to the south coast. In total, six Bf 110s and one Bf109 were shot down by the RAF fighters, including that of the leader Rubensdörffer who died along with his gunner Kretzer in the crash.

I had wanted to paint this scene for a long time as the combination of evening haze over London and pale grey Bf110s just had to make a striking image. I chose as my main subject the Bf110 of the Gruppe Technical Officer Koch as there are some nicely detailed photos of his crash landed aircraft to work from. I then had to work in the other elements to add drama and balance to the composition. One important point that came out of the early research was that the Bf110s quickly adopted a defensive circle at altitude, a common tactic for this type, rather than race for home individually at low level as I first assumed. Thus the action is set over Croydon with the 110s in the background climbing off target and forming the circle as the Hurricanes arrive.

The initial result can be seen above, a complex, conflicting mix of aircraft representing the chaos of the beginning of a deadly dogfight. A few months after completion, a regular collector of mine asked if I would consider making the picture less busy, as I had hinted at in an online video I'd made of the painting of this picture. We talked through the possibilities and agreed to make a few 'tweaks' to restore a bit of order! The final result can be seen to the left. I think both versions work in their own way but as for which is best, I'll let you decide!

COMBAT OVER CROYDON
Acrylic on linen, 30" x 20", 2010
In the collection of Neil T Bremer

43

Spitfire on my Tail

Fw. Ernst Arnold of 3/JG27 in his Messerschmitt Bf109E tries unsuccessfully to shake off RAF ace Brian Carbury near Canterbury on 30th August 1940. Carbury's 603 Squadron Spitfire eventually damaged Arnold's Bf109 badly enough for him to have to crash land near Faversham. The unfortunate German pilot was taken prisoner and his aircraft was put on display to the public in various locations to raise money for the war effort.

The scissors emblem behind the cockpit is believed to be a reference to a previous leader of 3 Staffel, Ulrich Scherer. With 'schere' being German for scissors and there being an 'r' added just under the bottom blade, the theory does seem to be reasonably valid!

I enjoyed painting this one. Everything went pretty smoothly but it's difficult to go wrong with these two classic fighters, especially with the Bf109's dominant yellow nose providing the main focal point. The yellow-nosed 109 has become almost obligatory in every Battle of Britain painting yet this tactical marking was only introduced in mid-August at around the same time that underwing roundels were re-introduced onto the RAF fighters. Whilst both markings really add to the visual appeal of a painting, if the scene depicted is before 12th August 1940 then they simply shouldn't be there.

The debate about artistic licence in aviation art has been going on for years with most artists choosing to ignore certain aspects of history to achieve a better or more pleasing composition. Unfortunately for me, I'm from the fundamentalist hard-core historian side of the debate, meaning that I have to work twice as hard to achieve decent, (albeit historically accurate), results!

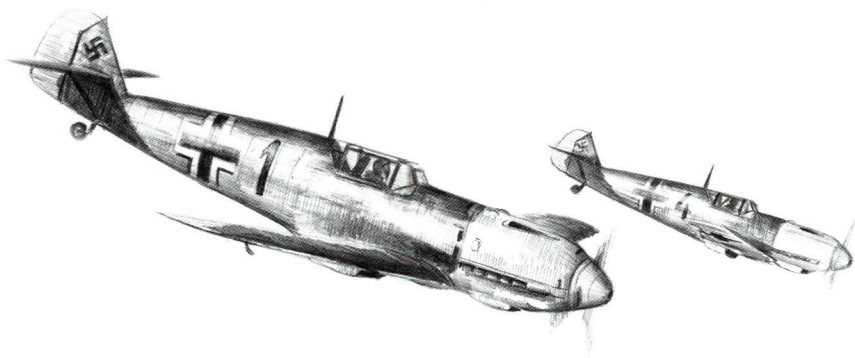

SPITFIRE ON MY TAIL
Acrylic on linen, 30" x 20", 2007
In the collection of Brian Carbury

MARK POSTLETHWAITE

DROGA DO NIEBA
Acrylic on linen, 48" x 20", 2011
In the collection of Nigel Szembel

Droga do Nieba

On 27th September 1940, 303 (Polish) Squadron was scrambled with 1 (Canadian) Squadron at 0845, initially to patrol Northolt at 15,000 feet and then to intercept a raid flying up the Thames Estuary. Flt Lt Athol Forbes, leading 303 Squadron in RF-O, had already lost radio contact with the Canadians when they suddenly changed course to fly parallel with the enemy formation. Forbes couldn't understand this so continued to head for the bombers, soon encountering some very accurate AA fire. Checking back over his shoulder he was somewhat startled to find he was on his own! The rest of 303 Squadron had spotted another bomber formation that he had not previously seen and were already engaging them, presuming that Forbes was returning to base with a technical problem. At the same time, Forbes observed to his horror a formation of Messerschmitt Bf109s diving out of the sun onto his unsuspecting pilots. Unable to raise anyone on his malfunctioning radio, he applied emergency boost and rushed towards the Bf109s in the hope he could somehow break up their attack before they struck.

The first Pole to spot the Bf109s was Jan Zumbach who gave a desperate warning to his fellow pilots. The Messerschmitts tore through the Polish formation at high speed with devastating results. Ludwik Paszkiewicz in RF-T and Tadeusz Andruszków in RF-J were both mortally hit and went down in flames over the countryside south-east of London. Walerian Żak in RF-S was also hit and forced to bale out of his burning Hurricane over Leatherhead. The other pilots managed to evade the initial onslaught and threw themselves into a general dogfight which saw them claim 11 enemy aircraft destroyed.

When the exhausted pilots landed back at Northolt around 10am, a total of five Hurricanes had either been destroyed or badly damaged, two pilots were dead and one in hospital with severe burns. Despite this, seven pilots were up on another patrol within a couple of hours and six others engaged the enemy again in the early afternoon, such was the relentless pace of the Battle of Britain at that time.

This painting started off as a demonstration piece to my daughter's primary school in Poland. I wanted to paint a subject that had a good story behind it so that the children would be able to find out more about what they saw. After considering many options I finally chose 303 Squadron on the morning of 27th September, as we could tell the full story of the 11 young pilots who went up that day. Each aircraft, pilot, serial number and position in formation is researched and identified. We even went to the extent of making sure the code letter style (there were two) and badge position was correct for each aircraft.

MARK POSTLETHWAITE '11

The Toby Spitfire

A pair of 303 (Polish) Squadron Spitfires head out on a coastal patrol in September 1941. The nearest Spitfire la R7162 was presented to the RAF by the Spitfire Fund on behalf of the Charrington Brewery. It was named 'Toby' after one of the company's famous ales and joined 411 (RCAF) Squadron in June 1941. Shortly afterwards it was damaged on landing and sent away for repair before returning to front-line duties with 303 and 306 (Polish) Squadrons in the autumn. By this stage it was obsolete for front-line operations so it ended its days with various OTUs, training the next generation of fighter pilots.

This painting was commissioned by Mitchells and Butlers the company that absorbed the Charrington brewery in the post-war years. The idea was to present the original painting to the Birmingham City Council to commemorate the brewery's Midland connections and the fact that thousands of Spitfires were built at nearby Castle Bromwich, (although Toby was inconveniently built at Southampton!)

The MD, having some Polish roots, was keen to display the Spitfire in the colours of 303 Squadron, but as it spent less than a month with the famous unit, we were pretty limited in what we could show it doing. In the end we opted for a coastal patrol which suited all concerned. They were based up near Liverpool at the time so although those cliffs look very much like the White Cliffs of Dover... (at the client's insistence), they are in fact the lesser known white cliffs of Birkenhead...!

Copies of this painting were subsequently framed and hung in every one of the company's Toby Carvery restaurants scattered around the UK. I ate in several but failed to secure even a 1% discount for my troubles!

THE TOBY SPITFIRE
Acrylic on canvas, 48" x 20", 2006
In the collection of Birmingham City Council

HEINKEL 111 UNITS
Acrylic on board, 15" x 15", 2011
In the collection of Roger Watts

Heinkel He111 Units in the West

On 14th August 1940 the Geschwaderkommodore of KG55, 44 year old Oberst Alois Stoeckl led a group of He111s to attack Liverpool. En-route to the target however, Stoeckl's bomber developed engine trouble and he was forced to turn back along with two other aircraft from the raid. As they searched for a decent target to leave their bombs with, an airfield appeared ahead, probably Middle Wallop in Hampshire. Just as they were lining up for the attack they were intercepted by Spitfires including that of 609 Squadron's David Crook. The combat was brief and Crook could only claim a 'damaged' as the He111s slipped back into the heavy cloud cover. Stoeckl's bomber however, had been badly hit and the aircraft crashed east of Salisbury at Dean Hill, claiming the life of Stoeckl and two other crew members.

For this painting, another piece of Osprey cover art, I chose a good angle on the He111 to show its classic lines. It also enabled me to use the colourful KG55 emblem to add a bit of colour to a grey day. The question of whether the Spitfire should have underwing roundels was a tricky one as the order had gone out to re-introduce them a couple of days before. However there is photographic evidence of a Spitfire shot down on 15th August without them so I left them off. No doubt some squadrons were quicker than others in applying the markings but at the height of the Battle I'd guess it took at least a week to apply in most cases.

A Stuka in my Sights

On 7th November 1940, Hurricanes of 249 Squadron were scrambled to intercept a heavy raid building in the Thames Estuary. Climbing above thick November haze and cloud, the RAF pilots saw nothing until the controllers finally realised that they were at least 14,000ft too high and the enemy aircraft were at sea level bombing a convoy!

249 tumbled down at speeds approaching 400mph and burst through the cloud straight into a gaggle of Junkers Ju87 Stukas. As Wing Commander Tom Neil, flying the C/O's Hurricane V7676 GN-J, was later to recall, "The first thing I saw was a big fat Stuka surging towards me at an unseemly rate, backwards!" All three airmen exchanged momentary glances at each other before being lost in the developing dogfight in which Tom Neil claimed one Ju87 and two Bf109s.

I have had the privilege to know Tom Neil and his wife Eileen for many years and have had many long and interesting chats about his wartime career. I decided that it was about time I painted him in action and asked him to suggest a day that he remembered more than most. 'Easy' he said, '7th November 1940'. I crashed on take-off in the morning, shot three aircraft down in the afternoon and then had to bale out in the evening after having my tail chopped off by the Station Commander!'

It seemed a reasonably interesting day (!) so we discussed the various options and ended up focusing on the afternoon combat. The one moment that caught my imagination immediately was his vision of a Stuka flying backwards towards him at great speed as he pulled out of his dive. He clearly remembered the startled expressions on the Stuka crewmen's faces as he whizzed by so I set about recreating this moment, the result of which you can see opposite.

A STUKA IN MY SIGHTS
Acrylic on canvas, 30" x 20", 2008
In the collection of Simon W Parry

Beaufighter over Paris

On 12th June 1942, a lone Beaufighter of 236 Squadron zoomed down the Champs Élysées at zero feet and dropped a French Tricolore over the Arc de Tromphe. An audacious act designed to boost morale amongst the French and to disrupt a planned German parade. The sortie was flown with great precision by Flight Lieutenant Ken Gatward and Sergeant George Fern and remains one of the most memorable single aircraft sorties of WWII.

Another cover commission from Aeroplane magazine, this time for its Bristol centenary edition. At first I wasn't so keen, after all, painting Paris from 100ft precluded the use of any handy clouds to hide the thousands of buildings! However I said I would give it some thought and after studying maps of the route I realised that I could probably hide most of the buildings with trees that lined the Champs Élysées. Suitably inspired by my labour saving discovery I knocked up a quick sketch and set to work on the final painting.

I needed to include the Eiffel Tower to show that it was Paris so again, a study of the map was called for to work out which way the aircraft would have been heading with the Tower in the background. Once all that was worked out, the painting went pretty smoothly and appeared on the cover as you can see here.

As is usually the case, the designers fiddled with the image a bit to make it fit the cover text. Note how the Eiffel Tower points past the nose on the painting but at the nose on the cover. I can happily live with things like that but I still haven't worked out quite why they removed the Tricolore, which was the whole point of the story in the first place!

Below: The final proposal sketch

BEAUFIGHTER OVER PARIS
Acrylic on board, 22" x 15", 2010
In the collection of Darryl Elliott

MARK POSTLETHWAITE '10

Beaufighter Aces of WWII

Flight Lieutenant John Cunningham and Sergeant Jimmy Rawnsley stalk a Heinkel 111 off the Dorset coast on 15th February 1941. After waiting for it to get sufficiently dark, Cunningham closed to firing range and shot the KG27 bomber down near Harberton.

This painting was commissioned for the cover of Osprey's Beaufighter Aces of WWII. The significant sentence in the crew's report for me was that they spotted the Heinkel as 'a tiny black speck against an opal curtain of light'. Having flown many times at dusk, I knew exactly what they meant and set about trying to re-create that intensely colourful twilight glow. This also solved that always tricky task of painting a black aircraft at night, in the dark with no lights on... probably being flown by a black cat...

BEAUFIGHTER ACES OF WWII
Acrylic on board, 15" x 11", 2007
Private collection

The Hewish Heinkel

A Heinkel He111 H-5 of III/KG26 is shot down by a Beaufighter of 604 Sqn on 4th April 1941 just south of Weston-Super-Mare.

Back in July 2009 I was invited along to the dig of an He111 bomber which crashed near Weston-Super-Mare in 1941. The excavation formed part of a TV documentary 'Dig 1940', first broadcast in September 2010. I decided to paint the aircraft high over the Bristol Channel just after it was hit by a Beaufighter of 604 Squadron. The aircraft was hit in the bomb bay and cockpit area and the burning incendiaries quickly set fire to the starboard wing. One of the interesting things about this Heinkel was that it had a catapult assisted take-off that evening due to its heavy load of fuel and bombs.

Below: The artist standing with one of the Heinkel's prop blades.

THE HEWISH HEINKEL
Acrylic on board, 22" x 15", 2009
In the collection of Neil T Bremer

Extraordinary Courage

Lieutenant Commander Eugene Esmonde DSO leads his heroic flight of six Swordfish against the might of the German Navy and Air Force during the Channel Dash, 12th February 1942. All six Swordfish were shot down and Esmonde was awarded a posthumous Victoria Cross. Only five of the 18 airmen survived. In the picture, Esmonde's Swordfish is seen in the distance on fire having lost its port lower mainplane and about to crash with no survivors. Behind him, Sub Lieutenant Brian Rose releases his torpedo as his aircraft is repeatedly hit. He ditched his aircraft shortly afterwards. In the foreground is the Swordfish of Sub Lieutenant Pat Kingsmill, already badly hit, about to release his torpedo. In the rear cockpit Leading Airman Don Bunce continues to fire and shout insults at the German fighters as they press home their attacks! The Focke Wulf 190s were forced to lower their flaps and undercarriage to enable them to slow down sufficiently to match the lumbering Swordfish's speed during the attack.

The third flight of three Swordfish led by Lieutenant J C Thompson then went into the attack. Within a few terrible minutes all three aircraft were destroyed and all nine men were killed.

This painting was commissioned for an Osprey book centre-spread. As such I had freedom to include action and combat, so I chose the dramatic final moments of the first wave as they were literally shot to pieces. There were many heroic deeds carried out in WWII, but these young men who steered their slow, canvas covered biplanes towards that inferno of flak, tracer and fighters, knowing that there was very little chance of survival, displayed a particularly extraordinary courage.

EXTRAORDINARY COURAGE
Acrylic on board, 22" x 15", 2008
In the collection of Rob Champion

Fiat CR.42 Aces

On 6th November 1940, Fiat CR.42s of 412ª Squadriglia intercepted a flight of Gloster Gladiators of 122 Squadron's 'K' flight over Abyssinia. The Italian pilots including Tenente Mario Visintini, seen here, achieved total surprise by attacking out of the sun and shot all three Gladiators down.

The nice thing about painting covers for Osprey is the variety of aircraft that I'm asked to paint. These two Italian examples are a case in point. The authors are usually experts in the subject and so can supply me with detailed references and each cover is meant to show a specific historical action rather than being generic. The final paintings often prove popular for subsequent book and magazine use as they illustrate scenes and campaigns rarely covered elsewhere.

53º Stormo

On 12th August 1942 fourteen Macchi C.202 Folgores of 153º Gruppo fought a running battle with Sea Hurricanes protecting the Pedestal convoy heading for Malta. During the combat, Maggiore Andrea Favini shot down a Sea Hurricane believed to be that of Sub Lt John Lucas.

FIAT CR.42 ACES
Acrylic on board, 15" x 11", 2009
In the collection of Egidio Gavazzi

53° STORMO
Acrylic on board, 15" x 11", 2010
In the collection of Paolo Ciabatti

American Spitfire Aces

Major Frank Hill of the 309th Fighter Squadron in Spitfire V ER187 WZ-C shoots down a Macchi C.202 in a combat over Tunis on 6th May 1943. This proved to be a very intense day of fighting for the 31st Fighter Group, making a claim for the largest number of enemy fighters destroyed by an American Fighter Group in a single day in North Africa.

Both of the paintings on these pages are of the immortal Spitfire. I've lost count of the number of Spitfires I've painted over the years but it must be nearing a hundred. The elliptical wing and slim fuselage make it almost too graceful to be a fighter, but a fighter it was, as many Axis pilots like the two seen here found out to their cost.

The painting on the left was commissioned for the cover of Osprey's American Spitfire Aces of WWII book and the one on the right for the November 2004 edition of US magazine Aviation History.

AMERICAN SPITFIRE ACES
Acrylic on board, 15" x 11", 2007
Private Collection

Wildcat Wade

Legendary American Ace Lance 'Wildcat' Wade shoots down a Messerschmitt Bf109F of JG53 over Tunisia on 1st March 1943.

L. C. Wade, (apparently his parents only gave him initials at birth!), joined the RAF via Canada in December 1940. His first tour of operations was with 33 Squadron in North Africa from late 1941 to September 1942. During this period he claimed 15 enemy aircraft destroyed. After a rest period back in the US, he returned to North Africa with 145 Squadron, initially as a Flight Commander but then as the C/O. At the end of his second tour he had achieved a tally of 25 victories making him the highest scoring American pilot who served only with the RAF.

Sadly on 12th January 1944, Wade was killed when his Auster communications aircraft crashed on take-off at Foggia, ending the remarkable life of a boy from the east hills of Texas.

WILDCAT WADE
Acrylic on board, 15" x 11", 2004
Private Collection

The Death of 'Strafer' Gott

On the afternoon of 7th August 1942 four Messerschmitt Bf109Fs of II/JG27 were on a 'freie jagd' patrol over Egypt when they spotted a lone Bristol Bombay transport aircraft flying at low level over the desert. After a first devastating firing pass from the fighters, the pilot of the Bombay, Sergeant 'Jimmy' James immediately force landed the aircraft onto the barren scrubland below and ordered an immediate evacuation of the aircraft. At this moment a second Messerschmitt swooped into attack and strafed the still moving Bombay, killing most of the passengers on board. The fatalities included Lieutenant General William Gott who had just been appointed commander of the 8th Army by Churchill, who was said to have wept openly when he heard the news.

This loss of the most senior British soldier to be killed by enemy fire in WWII, led to the hasty appointment of the little known Bernard Montgomery to replace Gott. 'Monty' as he became known, went on of course to lead the 8th Army to great successes at El Alamein and beyond, the hand of fate having given him the opportunity to become one of the most famous Generals of the war.

This painting was commissioned for Osprey's JG27 book in the Elite Units series. I chatted to the author John Weal about possible subjects and this one stood out clearly for its historical significance. By complete chance some years later I was introduced to an ex-RAF pilot who turned out to be none other than 'Jimmy' James the pilot of the Bombay and one of the only survivors of this event. We discussed the combat in great detail from his point of view and I believe that he had also spoken post-war to one of the Bf109 pilots. There is a theory that this may not have been such a 'chance' encounter and that maybe the Germans knew about Gott's presence on this aircraft. I promised Jimmy that I'd repaint the scene from his point of view and I'm ashamed to say that as yet, it's still on my to-do list. Hopefully it'll appear in volume three.

COMBAT OVER MALTA
Acrylic on board, 15" x 11", 2007
Private collection

THE DEATH OF 'STRAFER' GOTT
Acrylic on board, 15" x 11", 2007
Private collection

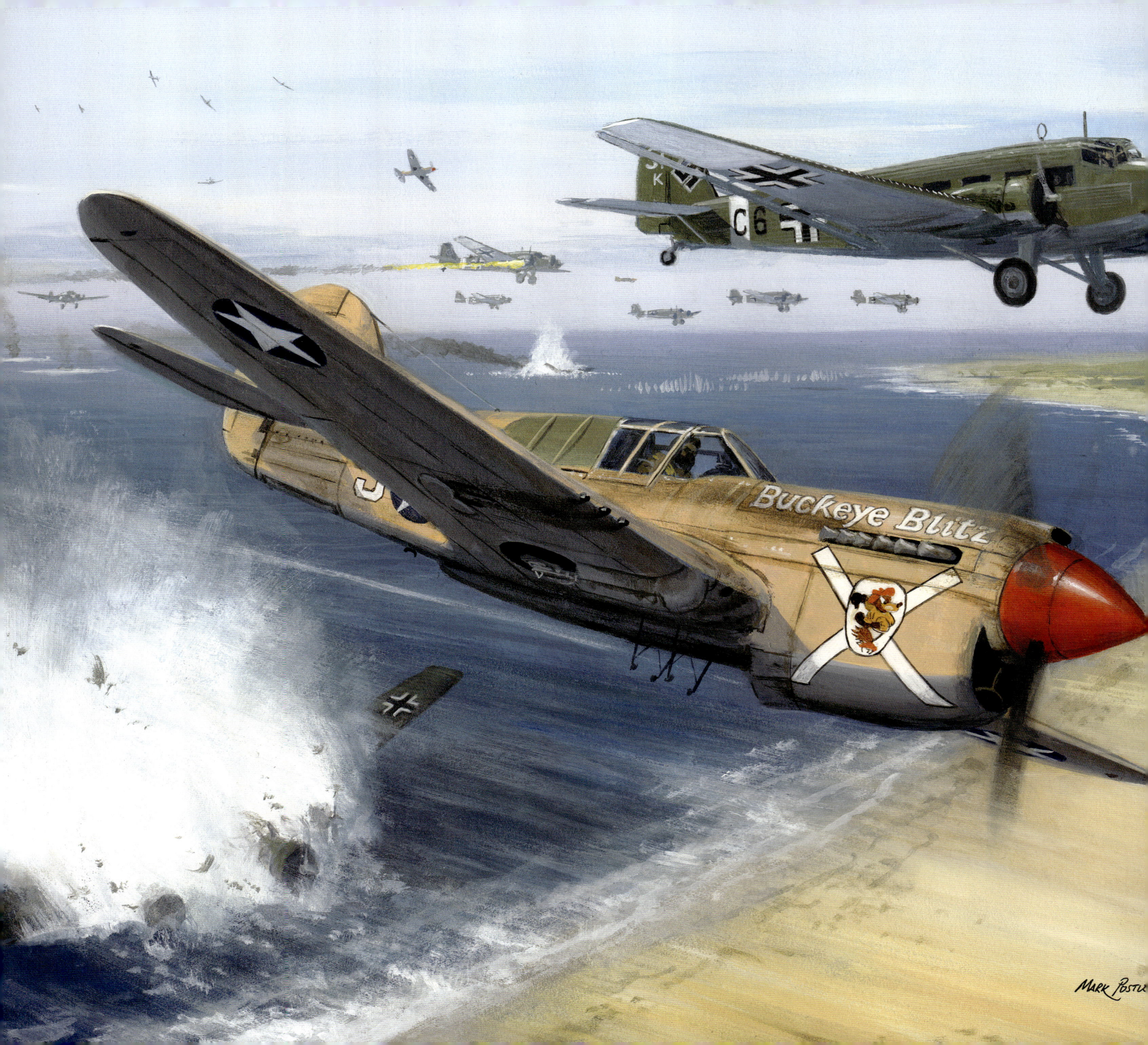

The Palm Sunday Massacre

By the middle of April 1943, the German position in North Africa was looking hopeless and the Luftwaffe was tasked with the urgent evacuation of as many troops as possible from Tunisia. On Sunday 18th April a large formation of over 70 Junkers Ju52 transport aircraft was spotted near Cape Bon by patrolling P-40s of the 57th Fighter Group. Captain James G Curl leading the American fighters in 'Buckeye Blitz' led the 48 P-40s down into attack as a handful of Bf109s tried to protect the lumbering transport aircraft. The ensuing combat saw the 57th Fighter Group claim no less than 76 aircraft destroyed for the loss of just six P-40s. Curl himself claimed two Ju52s, one Bf109 and two Ju52s damaged.

Four days later, another massed formation of some 20 German transports, this time the huge six-engined Me323, was spotted in the same area by Spitfires of 1 Squadron SAAF. Again a fighter escort of Bf109s and Macchi C.202s tried to protect the transports but again the German fighters were heavily outnumbered. In all, 14 Me323s were shot down into the sea along with several of their fighter escorts. These terrible losses forced the Germans to halt the daylight transport missions immediately thus disrupting significantly the flow of troops back to the Italian mainland. In the picture below, Lieutenant 'Robbie' Robinson in Spitfire Vc JG959 shoots down one of the Bf109 fighter escorts as another Spitfire closes in on an Me323 below.

SPITFIRE ACES OF NORTH AFRICA
Acrylic on board, 15" x 11", 2010
In the collection of Dave Robinson

THE PALM SUNDAY MASSACRE
Acrylic on board, 15" x 11", 2010
In the collection of Neil T Bremer

P-40 over Russia

Lieutenant Nikolai Kuznetsov of 436 IAP engages Bf109s in his P-40K during a Sturmovik escort mission on 26th December 1942 in the region of Velikiye Luki. Kuznetsov's P-40 was just one of over 2000 supplied to the Russians as part of the Lend-Lease agreements.

I-16 RATA ACES
Acrylic on board, 15" x 11", 2009
In the collection of John Birdsell

P-40 OVER RUSSIA
Acrylic on board, 15" x 11", 2006
In the collection of Neil T Bremer

Sturmovik Attack

Jnr Lt V P Aleksukhin and his gunner A D Gatayunov of the 617th ShAP attack German armoured vehicles during the Battle of Kursk in August 1943. Their IL-2 Sturmovik bore the name of Aleksandr Suvorov a famous Russian Field Marshal of the 18th Century.

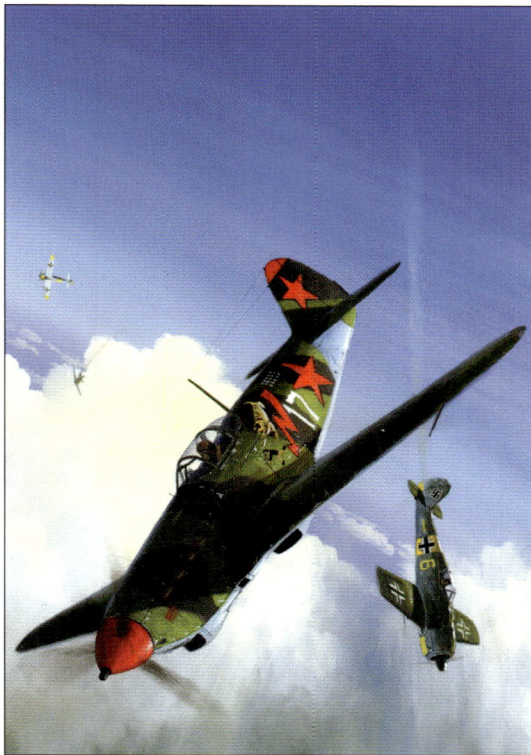

YAKOVLEV ACES
Acrylic on board, 15" x 11", 2004
Private Collection

STURMOVIK ATTACK
Acrylic on board, 15" x 11", 2007
Artist's Collection

Combat over Finland

A Focke Wulf Fw 189 of Aufkl.Gr. (H) 32 on an early morning reconnaissance mission, runs into trouble in the form of a formation of Soviet Hurricanes over Loukhi, Finland, 4th May 1943. The Hawker Hurricane was another Lend-Lease aircraft that saw extensive service with the Soviets during WWII. Re-armed with Soviet machine guns to ensure a constant supply of ammunition, the Soviet Hurricanes performed very well against sometimes far superior opposition.

In the painting below, a Hurricane Mk.IIB Z3768 'white 49', with the inscription 'For the All-Union Communist Party of Bolsheviks (V⦤Pb)' flown by Dmitriy Amosov shoots down a Bf109E of 14/JG77 near Murmansk on 15th December 1941.

SOVIET HURRICANE ACES OF WWII
Acrylic on board, 15" x 11", 2012
In the collection of John Birdsell

COMBAT OVER FINLAND
Acrylic on canvas, 30" x 20", 2005
Private Collection

Moscow Defender

Captain Mark Gallay a test pilot from the Flight Testing Institute shoots down a Dornier Do17Z of 9/KG3 during the first raid on Moscow on 21st July 1941. He was serving with the hastily formed 2nd Separate Fighter Air Squadron of the Moscow Air Defence Forces at the time alongside fellow test pilots. The Dornier flown by Lt Kurt Kuhn crashed shortly afterwards.

MOSCOW DEFENDER
Acrylic on board, 15" x 11", 2011
Artist's Collection

Stuka over Stalingrad

Leutnant Heinz Jungclaussen Staffelkapitän of 6/StG2 dives his Junkers Ju87 'Stuka' onto a Soviet target near the 'Red October' iron works at Stalingrad in the winter of 1942. Jungclaussen went on to fly and survive over 1000 Stuka missions before taking a spell as an instructor in early 1944. He returned to operations in November of the same year flying Focke Wulf 190s with 3/SG4, but his vast experience stood little chance against increasingly overwhelming odds. On Boxing Day 1944 he was killed in action south of Koblenz in a combat with RAF Typhoons.

STUKA OVER STALINGRAD
Acrylic on board, 15" x 11", 2008
Private Collection

Operation Leader

Dauntlesses and Wildcats operating from USS Ranger attack German shipping in Bodø harbour on 4th October 1943. This little known action was the first time that US carrier based aircraft had appeared over occupied Norway.
The attacking aircraft were divided into two waves. A Northern Attack Group consisting of 20 SBD Dauntless dive-bombers with an escort of eight F4F Wildcat fighters were directed to attack shipping and shore installations near Bodø. A Southern Attack Group consisting of ten TBF Avengers and six F4F Wildcats was directed toward Sandnessjöen.

The aircraft attacked several ships, sinking at least two and damaging the others, for the loss of four airmen killed and three taken prisoner. It was the first taste of action for many of the airmen from Air Group 4 whose Commanding Officer Cdr. Joseph A. Ruddy summed up thus;

"LEADER was definitely an excellent training exercise for CAG-4. We went in as many boys and came out as many men."

My wife and I had visited Bodø on a research trip back in 1999 and had fallen in love with the peace and tranquillity of the area. Admittedly it was mid-summer with the midnight sun beautifully illuminating the hills and mountains even at 3am. We may have formed a slightly different opinion if we had been there in January!
Whilst I was there, I first heard about Operation Leader and determined to find out a bit more about this very unusual mission. Luckily there was a superb website covering Air Group 4's entire wartime exploits, www.airgroup4.com, with dozens of photos taken during the mission itself. With the help of this and Norwegian sources, we managed to put together this composition of a pair of SBD Dauntlesses peeling off to dive bomb shipping with Bodø nestling in the hills beyond. The photo below shows the scene a few seconds before from a viewpoint to the right of the painting.

OPERATION LEADER
Acrylic on canvas, 42" x 28", 2007
In the collection of the Norwegian Armed Forces

MARK POSTLETHWAITE GAvA '07

AICHI 99 'VAL' UNITS
Acrylic on board, 15" x 11", 2010
In the collection of Roger Watts

Aichi 99 'Val' Units

Lt Cdr Kakuichi Takahashi rolls his Aichi Type 99 Carrier Bomber over Ford Island to begin the attack on Pearl Harbor, 0755hrs, 7th December 1941. The 'Day of Infamy' is about to begin.

P-36 Hawk Aces of WWII

19 year old 2Lt Harry Brown engages the Japanese aircraft attacking Pearl Harbor on the morning of 7th December 1941. Still wearing his pyjama top after a hasty scramble, Brown managed to shoot down two B5N torpedo bombers in his old Curtiss P-36 Hawk fighter.

CATALINA UNITS OF THE PACIFIC WAR
Acrylic on board, 15" x 11", 2006
Private Collection

P-36 HAWK ACES OF WWII
Acrylic on board, 15" x 11", 2008
Artist's collection

Buffalo Aces
of WWII

On 13th December 1941 Buffalos of 453 Squadron RAAF flew almost round the clock, combating wave after wave of incoming hostile bombers during the Japanese invasion of Malaya. Flight Lieutenant Doug Vanderfield flying Buffalo AN185 TD-V had trouble with raising his landing gear after take-off and had to go into combat with everything hanging down. Despite this he managed to claim two bombers and one dive-bomber destroyed including the Ki-48 'Lily' seen here in the painting.

BUFFALO ACES OF WWII
Acrylic on board, 15" x 11", 2009
In the collection of Neil T Bremer

Hurricane
Aces 41-45

On the morning of 6th February 1942, pilots of 135 Squadron were scrambled to intercept a Japanese raid headed for Rangoon. Leading the six Hurricanes was 27 year old Pilot Officer Jack Storey in Z5659 WK-C. The Australian pilot soon spotted a formation of Ki-27 'Nates' and led his squadron into attack, quickly despatching one 'Nate' before being engaged by two more from behind. In the dogfight that followed, Storey shot down another Ki-27 and claimed two more as probables.

When I did this painting, little did I imagine that the pilot would end up staying in our house in Poland for a few days with his wife and daughter! Jack or 'Uncle Jack' as he is now known to our kids has spent most of his life globetrotting with his lovely wife Heather. Despite both being in their nineties they contacted us and said they would be 'passing our way' from Austria to Warsaw and wondered if they could rest their legs for a bit! In the end they stayed three days with us and were marvellous company. Jack loved the painting and really felt that I had captured the scene as he remembered it. The only criticism he had was that I had painted the spinner black and he clearly remembered it being a plum colour. I duly changed it and am now satisfied that I've created a lasting tribute to lovely old Uncle Jack, one of the most remarkable men I've ever met.

HURRICANE ACES 41-45
Acrylic on board, 15" x 11", 2006
Private Collection

Ki-43 Oscar Aces of WWII

On 31st March 1943, eight combat veterans of the 50th Sentai took off in their Ki-43 'Oscars' for a strike against the Allied airfield at Pataga. Having strafed the airfield, the fighters reformed and waited at 19,000ft for the RAF fighters to respond. Soon ten Hurricanes of 135 Squadron were spotted climbing to intercept and the Japanese fighters fell on them before they had the chance to reach their height.

In the ensuing combat the Japanese pilots claimed 8 Hurricanes destroyed without loss to themselves. Post war research shows that only 3 Hurricanes were destroyed and one badly damaged but it was still a grim day for the RAF and a clear sign that the Japanese fighters were still a potent force.

Ki-43 OSCAR ACES OF WWII
Acrylic on board, 15" x 11", 2008
Artist's Collection

McGuire in Trouble

Leading 475th Fighter Group Ace 1Lt Tom McGuire runs into trouble over Oro Bay on 17th October 1943. Facing ever increasing odds, McGuire was forced to bale-out of his crippled P-38 Lightning into the sea. Luckily for him, he was rescued by a Navy PT boat some 30 minutes later.

McGUIRE IN TROUBLE
Acrylic on board, 15" x 11", 2006
In the collection of Neil T Bremer

CHENNAULT'S SHARKS
Acrylic on board, 15" x 11", 2008
In the collection of Neil T Bremer

Chennault's Sharks

P-51A Mustangs and P-40K Warhawks of the 76th Fighter Squadron, 23rd Fighter Group engage Ki-43s of the 11th and 25th Sentais over Suichuan airfield, China on 27th December 1943. The 76th Fighter Squadron's new C/O, Captain John S Stewart, flying his P-51 'Lynn' claimed one Ki-43 as a probable and the squadron as a whole claimed five enemy aircraft as destroyed.

Anti-Kamikaze Aces of WWII

Lt. Chico Freeman of VF-84 flying Corsair no. 133 shoots down a Kawanishi N1K1-J 'George' fighter about 75 miles north of Okinawa on 17th April 1945.

ANTI-KAMIKAZE ACES CF WWII
Acrylic on board, 15" x 11", 2012
Artist's Collection

Hellcats!

Cat's teeth marked Hellcats of VF-27 in action over the Pacific in mid-1944.

This is the original art for a computer game featuring Hellcats of VF-27 in action. The brief for this commission was to squeeze as much action into it as possible, a very rare brief in these pc days. As such, this painting is probably unique as it is the sort of scene I used to doodle on my school books when I was 12!

American Night Fighter Aces

Major R Bruce Porter, the C/O of VMF(N)-542 shoots down a Mitsubishi G4M 'Betty' off the northern coast of Okinawa on 15th June 1945, his second victory of the night which made him a five victory Ace.

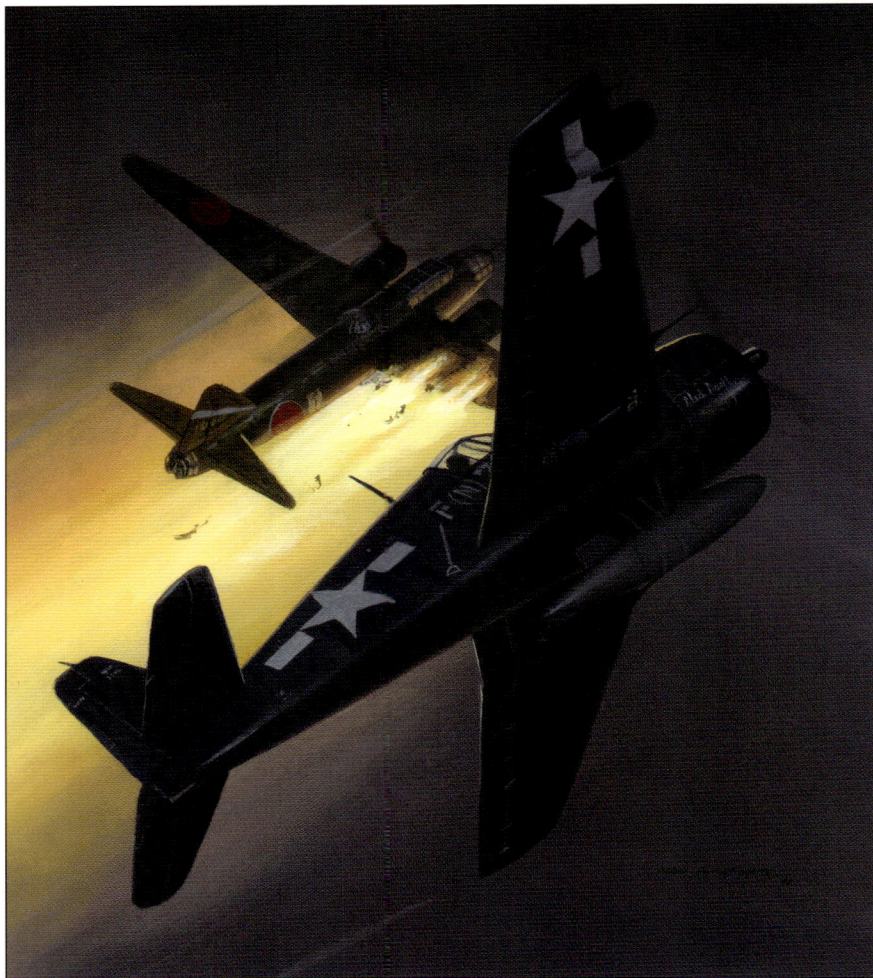

AMERICAN NIGHT FIGHTER ACES
Acrylic on board, 15" x 11", 2009
Artist's Collection

HELLCATS!
Acrylic on board, 20" x 13", 2011
Artist's Collection

MARK POSTLETHWAITE '11

Malta Spitfire Aces

Sergeant George 'Screwball' Beurling, one of WWII's most famous fighter Aces in action on 27th July 1942 over Malta. On this day he claimed four fighters destroyed and two damaged, contributing to his eventual total of 31 victories, 1 shared and 9 damaged.

MALTA SPITFIRE ACES
Acrylic on board, 15" x 11", 2008
Private Collection

Tragedy over Sicily

On the night of 11th July 1943 a large force of C-47 troop carriers taking part in Operation Husky 2 was fired upon by the US invasion fleet just off the coast of Sicily with tragic results. Over 20 C-47s were shot down with the loss of hundreds of men. C-47 41-38704 'Geronimo' was hit repeatedly before colliding with a jettisoned parapack which ripped through the fuselage causing severe damage. Despite this, pilots Captain James R Farris and 2Lt Joseph P Baxter managed to steer their crippled aircraft back to Tunisia where it was declared a total write-off.

TRAGEDY OVER SICILY
Acrylic on board, 15" x 11", 2007
Private Collection

Prepare for Ditching!

Warrant Officer Paul M. Wheeler of Coastal Command was posted to Ein Shemer, near Tel Aviv, in late 1944 to train new crews destined for anti-U-Boat patrols in the Eastern Mediterranean on Wellington XIIIs. On 3rd November, W/O Wheeler was given a crew fresh out from the UK and told to take them on a nav patrol exercise. They set off in clear weather; the wind was fresh and there was no moon.

After about an hour one of the new crew tapped W/O Wheeler on the shoulder: 'Skipper – have you seen the port engine? It's on fire.' Wheeler handed over to the P2 and went to investigate. Flames were pouring out of the engine nacelle. Returning to his seat, he quickly tried to feather the prop, but to no avail.
Turning for home on just the starboard engine, things got much worse just a few minutes later when it too spluttered and failed. Wheeler gave the order: 'Dinghy, dinghy, prepare for ditching' and jettisoned the cockpit roof.

In almost total darkness, Wheeler eased his way down gently towards the breaking waves below. When the Wellington finally hit the sea it hit the water hard and began to sink immediately. Wheeler found himself sinking with the aircraft, unable to release his harness. He blacked out, and his next memory is of finding himself on the surface, with his hands scratched to ribbons; unconsciously, he must have torn himself free while the aircraft was going down.

There were two other crew members in the sea and a lot of wreckage, but no dinghy. The night was pitch-black and the waves were breaking down onto the swimmers, whose Mae Wests were keeping them afloat. For some reason Wheeler removed the battery from his floating torch and tucked it inside his shirt pocket. It was difficult for the survivors to stay together in these conditions. Twice Wheeler swam off to bring back the Wireless Operator/ AG, who couldn't swim. On the third occasion the man was lifeless and there was nothing that could be done for him.

The two survivors tried to keep going with puzzles and quiz questions. After some time a Wellington flew overhead. Wheeler put the battery back into his floating torch and sent an SOS. The Wellington flew overhead, very low, and sent a message: 'Help coming – take care'. Then a second message: 'Have to go – short of fuel'.

Some time later (it turned out to be 10 hours) the swimmers heard the chug-chug of an engine and a searchlight swept the sea around them. A voice said: 'Can't see anyone'. Then they were spotted and the air-sea rescue launch drifted down to their position. A net was lowered over the side and crew-members pulled the two survivors out, in Wheeler's own words, 'like dead fish'.

This painting was commissioned by Adrian Wheeler for his father Paul's 86th birthday in October 2008. Sadly Paul Wheeler died shortly afterwards but at least had the pleasure of seeing this painting recording one of his most memorable nights. The story told here was written by Paul after conversations with his father and appeared as a feature in the April 2009 edition of Aeroplane Magazine.

PREPARE FOR DITCHING!
Acrylic on canvas, 30" x 20", 2008
In the collection of the Wheeler family

MARK POSTLETHWAITE '08

Second Chance

Lieutenant Johansen and Sub-Lieutenant Humlen in Mosquito HP864 3-H of 333 (Norwegian) Squadron attack U-998 off Sognefjorden on 16th June 1944. The U-boat was badly damaged but managed to limp back to Bergen where it was written off.

Sunderland Strike

A 461 Squadron RAAF Sunderland attacks a Type VII U-boat in the Atlantic, mid 1943.

This painting was commissioned for the cover of Aeroplane magazine (left) and is mainly a study of light and shade. The lovely large white hull of the Sunderland is an artist's dream, allowing us to play with all sorts of shadows and weathering upon it.

SUNDERLAND STRIKE
Acrylic on canvas, 22" x 15", 2008
In the collection of Neil T Bremer

SECOND CHANCE
Acrylic on canvas, 42" x 28", 2005
In the collection of the Norwegian Armed Forces

MARK POSTLETHWAITE GAvA 05

Operation Steinbock

Heinkel He 177s of KG40 fly low on a transit flight in preparation for an operation over England during Operation Steinbock, early 1944. The He177 was remarkable in that it was actually a four engined heavy bomber. The four engines were twinned in each nacelle, driving a huge propeller. Not surprisingly, this type suffered from engine problems as a result and a man with an extinguisher was always on hand at start up!

Mosquito Aces of WWII

On the night of 25th November 1944, American pilot Lieutenant A A Harrington and his RAF navigator Flying Officer D G Tongue achieved a triple victory in one night, shooting down three Ju88G night fighters in the space of just 18 minutes. The 410 (RCAF) Squadron airmen were operating over Germany from their base in northern France and used mobile ground radar to guide them to the first victim shown here.

MOSQUITO ACES OF WWII
Acrylic on board, 15" x 11", 2006
Private Collection

OPERATION STEINBOCK
Acrylic on canvas, 30" x 20", 2008
Private Collection

The Amiens Raid

Mosquitos of 487 (NZ) Squadron, led by Wing Commander 'Black' Smith in LR333 EG-R, drop the first bombs on Amiens Prison during the famous raid of 18th February 1944. Smith scored a direct hit with his delayed action bombs, blowing a big hole in the front wall of the prison. In the background, aircraft of the second wave can be seen commencing an unplanned 180° orbit having arrived in the target area too close to the first wave. At the rear of this formation is Group Captain Percy Pickard the overall leader of the raid who planned to go in last to assess whether the third wave needed to be brought in to bomb. Unfortunately an FW190 of JG26 flown by Fw. Wilhelm Mayer latched onto Pickard's Mosquito during the orbit and shot its tail section off. Pickard and his navigator 'Bill' Broadley stood no chance of survival as their Mosquito dived into the ground near St Gratien. Both are now buried in a cemetery just a few hundred yards from the prison itself.

The Amiens prison raid has always been famous for its epic attempt to free hundreds of condemned prisoners awaiting execution. However when my book publishing company received a French manuscript that proved there were no such condemned prisoners, we had to investigate further. After two years of work and further research, we finally felt confident enough to publish 'The Amiens Raid - Secrets Revealed' which basically points to the whole raid being part of Operation Fortitude, a monumental deception plan to keep German Forces away from the D-Day beaches in Normandy. This takes nothing away from the aircrews, who knew nothing of the deception. In fact the book emphasises just how well the raid was carried out. Once published, and having visited Amiens and Pickard's crash site, I knew I had to paint my version of the raid which you can see here. I've tried to tell the story by including the second wave in the distance which includes Percy Pickard, the remaining two Mosquitos of the first wave swinging north to attack from the north-west, and a lone Typhoon escort above to symbolise the lack of significant fighter escort due to bad weather, which probably cost Pickard his life.

THE AMIENS RAID
Acrylic on linen, 42" x 22", 2011
Private Collection, New Zealand.

Viermot Aces

Feldwebel Albert Palm of 3/JG4 breaks off from his attack on a B-24 Liberator of the 44th Bomb Group over Ploesti, Rumania, during Operation Tidal Wave on 1st August 1943.

Close Combat

Feldwebel Wilhelm Hopfensitz of IV/JG3 closes in on a B-17 of the 838th BS over Belgium, 24th December 1944 in his heavily armoured Sturmgruppen Focke Wulf 190.

VIERMOT ACES
Acrylic on board, 15" x 11", 2011
In the collection of Neil T Bremer

CLOSE COMBAT
Acrylic on board, 15" x 11", 2005
In the collection of Neil T Bremer

A-26 Invader Units of WWII

Lieutenant Lou Prucha's A26B Invader 'Sugar Baby' comes under intense anti-aircraft fire on a mission to bomb an ordinance depot at Unna, Germany on 16th February 1945.

A-26 INVADER UNITS
Acrylic on board, 15" x 11", 2009
In the collection of Rick Prucha

Bellagambi in Combat

On 8th February 1945 the 2nd Gruppo Caccia (Fighter Group) composed of Messerschmitt Me109Gs from the 4th, 5th and 6th Squadriglia (Squadron) of the ANR – 24 aircraft in total – took off from the airfield in Osoppo (Udine) and intercepted over north eastern Italy a group of B-25 Mitchell bombers from the 310th Bomb Group based in Corsica. Seven B-25s were shot down by the Italian Me 109s. Major Mario Bellagambi (Yellow 1) and Captain Ugo Drago claimed one B -25 each.

BELLAGAMBI IN COMBAT
Acrylic on board. 15" x 11", 2011
In the collection of Paolo Ciabatti

Combat over Budapest

First Lieutenant Grover Siems of the 4th Fighter Group shoots a Messerschmitt Me109 off the tail of Captain Howard Hively during a hectic combat over Budapest on 2nd July 1944. Seconds later, Siems was himself wounded and his Mustang 'Gloria III' badly damaged by another Me109 in the whirling mass of fighters. Despite his extensive injuries, Siems managed to guide his crippled Mustang down to Foggia in Italy, where after landing he sat unnoticed, too weak to move from blood loss until he managed to fire his guns to attract attention. When help finally came he was initially thought to be dead!

The P-51 Mustang is a joy to paint and is one of the few aircraft that looks good from nearly every angle including the rear. That's why, with 'Combat over Budapest', I chose a rear view so that the viewer feels part of the large turning combat that took place on that day. Unfortunately it meant that I couldn't use the 4th FG's red nose to good advantage, but I did manage to use the red and yellow chequered noses of the 457th FG to provide a focal point for the painting below. This time the opposition is in the form of FW190s over Holland on 18th September 1944 and the pilot is Lieutenant Gerald Tyler of the 364th Fighter Squadron in 'Little Duckfoot'.

MUSTANG ACES OF THE 357TH FG
Acrylic on board, 15" x 11", 2011
Artist's Collection

COMBAT OVER BUDAPEST
Acrylic on board, 15" x 11", 2008
Private Collection

MARK POSTLETHWAITE '08

Defence of the Reich Aces

Oberleutnant Gerhard Vogt of II/JG26 flying a Focke Wulf 190D-9 fights his last battle against American P-51 Mustangs near Aachen on 14th January 1945. He never returned from this mission.

Hartmann's Last Victory

The highest scoring fighter pilot in history, Erich Hartmann shoots down his last victim on 8th May 1945 in his Messerschmitt Me109K of JG52 over Brno. This was his 1405th combat mission and his 352nd confirmed victory in a truly remarkable career.

DEFENCE OF THE REICH ACES
Acrylic on board, 5" x 11", 2010
In the collection of Neil T Bremer

HARTMANN'S LAST VICTORY
Acrylic on board, 15" x 11", 2007
Private collection

A Norwegian Hero

Wing Commander Rolf Arne Berg leads the Norwegian Wing in his personal Supermarine Spitfire IX on a dive bombing mission near Dunkirk, winter 1944. The Norwegian markings on the wings and rudder were unique to this aircraft and only applied for a short period as Berg tried unsuccessfully to get High Command to allow the Norwegian units within the RAF to wear their national colours as the Free French squadrons were then doing. This request was turned down and by January 1945 his aircraft had been repainted back to standard RAF markings.

On 3rd February 1945, Berg was due to head home after a long operational tour. With his bags already packed he decided to fly one more mission that day, which turned out to be his last. His Spitfire was seen to lose a wing during a low level attack on a Luftwaffe airfield and Berg was killed instantly in the ensuing crash.

The Spitfire was a bit too delicate for ground-attack work, unlike the Hawker Typhoon (seen below) which was of a far more rugged construction and could carry rockets and bombs to go along with its four powerful 20mm cannon.

TYPHOON WINGS OF 2ND TAF
Acrylic on board, 15" x 11", 2010
In the collection of Darryl Elliott

A NORWEGIAN HERO
Acrylic on Canvas 42" x 28", 2009
In the Collection of the Norwegian Armed Forces

MARK POSTLETHWAITE '09

JG7 NOWOTNY
Acrylic on board, 15" x 11", 2008
In the collection of Neil T Bremer

JG7 'Nowotny'

Major Theodor Weissenberger, Commanding Officer of JG7, dives through a formation of B-17s of the 483rd Bomb Group on 22nd March 1945 in his Messerschmitt Me262 jet fighter. Within moments he shot down one of the B-17s contributing to the twelve bombers shot down by JG7 on this sortie.

Surprise Attack

The original cover art for Osprey's Messerschmitt Me262 Kampfgeschwader Units depicting Oberfeldwebel Hermann Wieczorek of 2/KG 51 attacking British vehicles near Bree, Belgium on 17th December 1944.

SURPRISE ATTACK
Acrylic on board, 15" x 11", 2012
In the collection of Jon Birdsell

Attacked by Jets

Messerschmitt Me262s of I/JG7 tear through a formation of Lancasters and Halifaxes heading for Hamburg on 31st March 1945. The Me262 was not only much faster than any Allied fighter, it also packed a heavy punch with its four Mk108 30mm cannon in the nose. A short burst from these guns could rip an aircraft to pieces. The Lancaster in the top right of the painting, PA226 AL-H of 429 Squadron had a huge hole blown in its starboard wing, luckily missing the outer wing fuel tank by inches. She managed to limp home unlike eight Lancasters and three Halifaxes that would never return from this raid.

The photo below shows PA226 after she returned from this mission.

ATTACKED BY JETS
Acrylic on Canvas 30" x 20", 2006
Private Collection

MARK POSTLETHWAITE 06

Veterans

A young Lancaster crew arrive at their aircraft in preparation for an operational sortie over Germany. This generic but faithfully detailed scene is designed to be a tribute to all those unsung crews of Main-Force who went about their thankless task, night after night, in the full knowledge that statistically, they probably wouldn't survive their tour of 30 ops.

Welcome to a special section devoted to my favourite subject, the Avro Lancaster.

This painting had been in my head for many years, my concept was to try to evoke the fear and grim determination that each man must have felt as they forced themselves to embark upon another op. This is an experienced 'veteran' crew, possibly with only a few ops left, each man involved in his own thoughts, just doing his job now, hoping to get it over with as soon as possible.

The Lancaster too is a veteran, engine cowlings heavily streaked with the pale exhaust deposits, paint chipped, panels dented, yet probably only a few months old. Will they return in the morning? We don't know, and most importantly they didn't either. But still they went night after night, conquering their personal fears in the hope and belief that their efforts would help bring a swift end to the war. Over 55,000 of them died as a result, the majority of them in their early twenties, veterans in every sense apart from age.

I read a quote by Robert Louis Stevenson once which seemed to sum up the character of those brave young men of RAF Bomber Command. It simply reads;

Keep your fears to yourself, but share your courage with others

VETERANS
Acrylic on linen 48" x 20", 2011
Private Collection, New Zealand

Lancaster over Bergen

Lancaster WS-X of IX Squadron turns away from the target area after dropping a Tallboy bomb on the U-boat pens at Bergen, Norway on 12th January 1945. Bomb-aimer Dennis Nolan clearly remembered seeing the effect of a Tallboy penetrating the thick concrete roof of the pens. He likened it to a Roman Candle where the Tallboy drilled a hole through the concrete then exploded inside, sending a spout of flame up through the hole and a cloud of debris out the front of the pens.

LANCASTER OVER BERGEN
Acrylic on canvas, 22" x 14", 2005
Private Collection

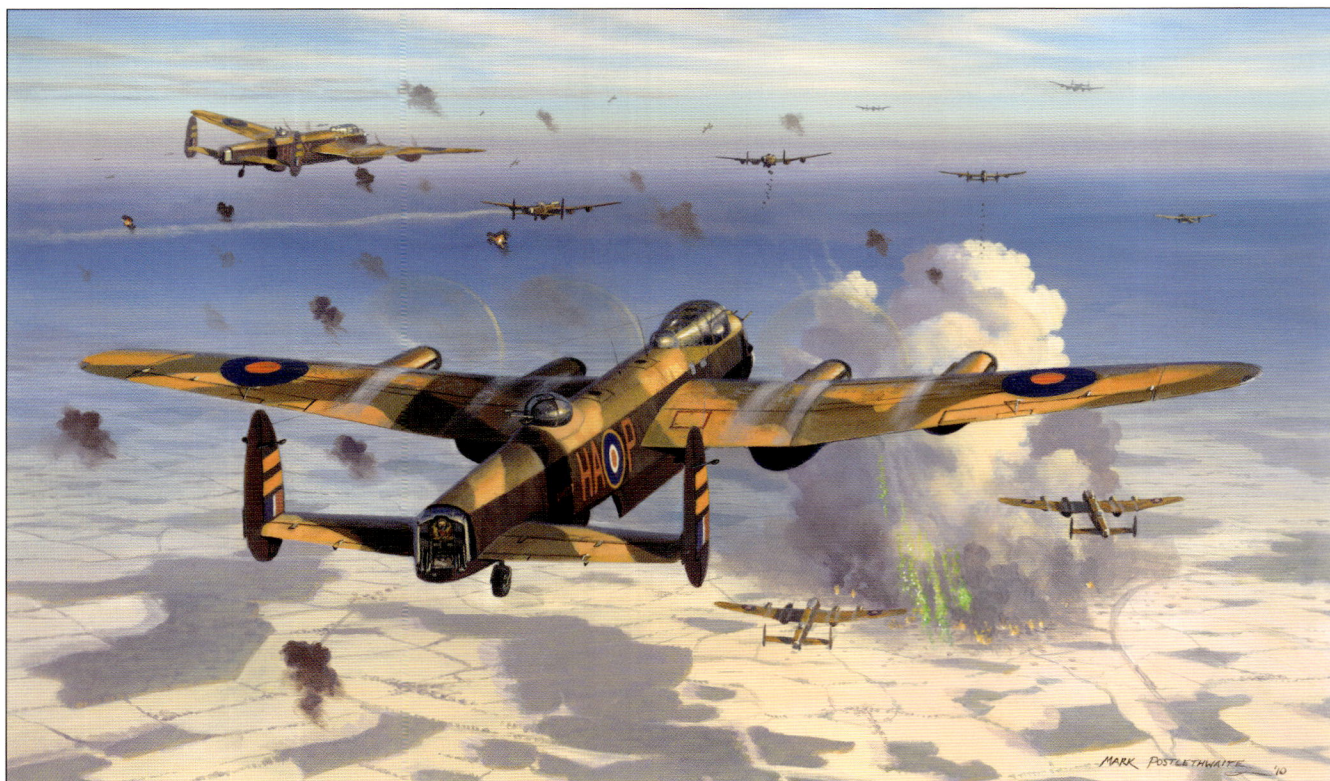

Lancasters over St Vith

A large force of Lancasters and Halifaxes of RAF Bomber Command including HA-P of 218 Squadron carry out a precision bombing attack on St Vith, 26th December 1944.

This painting was commissioned by the son of the rear-gunner who can be seen in his very cold 'office' wearing his lucky scarf for warmth!

LANCASTERS OVER ST VITH
Acrylic on canvas, 22" x 14", 2010
In the collection of Mark Laity

DAMBUSTERS - SETTING COURSE
Acrylic on canvas, 30" x 16", 2008
Private Collection

Dambusters - Setting Course

Wing Commander Guy Gibson leads his section out over Lincolnshire at the beginning of Operation Chastise, the Dambuster Raid of 16/17th May 1943.

Over the next few pages you'll find a selection of paintings featuring the famous Dambuster Raid. This raid has been of particular interest to me for many years and during the course of my research, I've tried to get as many details as accurate as possible. One of the biggest factors in the raid was the position of the moon. It was rising ahead of them on the outbound flight, making low level flight over water very difficult and during the attack on the Möhne it was off the port beam. I've seen many paintings of the Lancasters outbound with the moon behind them, which would mean they're flying back home(!) and attacking the Möhne with the moon behind them, which probably would have made them easy meat for the flak gunners. It is of course up to the artist to decide if these details are important, but for me they are crucial.

DAMBUSTERS - A MOMENT IN HISTORY
Acrylic on linen, 42" x 20", 2009
Private Collection, New Zealand

Dambusters
A Moment in History

Just a few minutes before the previous painting, Wing Commander Guy Gibson leads his section on take off from Scampton at the beginning of Operation Chastise. The full moon which would light their attack can be seen rising in the east as the setting sun illuminates the Lancasters with its final rays.

In the car below on Ermine Street, an off duty bomber crew head for Lincoln, oblivious to the fact that history is being made above their heads by those odd looking Lancs.

Of the three Lancasters seen here, AJ-M flown by John Hopgood, was shot down over the target (below) and AJ-P flown by Mick Martin was damaged by flak but returned safely along with AJ-G, Gibson's aircraft.

HOPGOOD'S LAST MOMENTS
Acrylic on board 15" x 11", 2009
Private Collection, New Zealand

Dambusters
Dusk Departure

And also just a few minutes after the previous painting, Squadron Leader 'Dinghy' Young leads his section on take off from Scampton at the beginning of Operation Chastise. On the skyline in the distance stands Lincoln Cathedral, a familiar beacon for many returning bomber crews.

Of the three Lancaster seen here Young's AJ-A was shot down on the way home killing all on board, the other two, AJ-J flown by Flt Lt David Maltby and AJ-L flown by Flt Lt David Shannon both returned safely although Maltby and his crew were killed just 4 months later.

I was commissioned to paint this shortly after I painted the scene on the previous page. The client wanted something very similar so I opted to show the second vic of three aircraft taking off behind Gibson. By this time I had also uncovered extra detail on the layout of Scampton at the time, so I was able to raise the viewpoint by about 50ft to show more of the airfield. This is something that I had wanted to do with the first painting, but because I didn't have the information I wasn't prepared to guess.

DAMBUSTERS - DUSK DEPARTURE
Acrylic on linen, 42" x 20", 2009
In the collection of Robin McIntyre

Dambusters
The Opening Shots

Wing Commander Guy Gibson makes the first bombing run of Operation Chastise at 00.28hrs on 17th May 1943 at the Möhne dam in Germany. With the other Lancasters holding in a racetrack pattern to the south-west, all eyes were on AJ-G as it got lower and lower over the water. Eventually its spotlights converged on the surface of the water, meaning they were just 60ft high, the optimum height to drop the Upkeep mine. John Pulford the Flight Engineer kept the speed at 220mph whilst Gibson kept the aircraft straight and level. Meanwhile in the nose turret, George Deering hosed the defences with 100% tracer to try to keep the gunners' heads down. Despite this tracer from both flak towers on the dam came uncomfortably close.

At approximately 470 yards from the target, bomb aimer Fred Spafford released the 'bouncing bomb' and a legend was formed. Although Gibson's Upkeep missed the target, others didn't and two dams were breached that night. The cost was high however, eight Lancasters failed to return that morning and 56 men were missing, only three of which were still alive.

DAMBUSTERS - THE OPENING SHOTS
Acrylic on linen, 48" x 20", 2007
Private Collection, New Zealand

The American Dambuster

Flight Lieutenant Joe McCarthy and his crew attack the Sorpe Dam at around 00.40hrs on 17th May 1943. McCarthy had been forced to change aircraft at the last moment when his regular Lancaster Q 'Queenie' developed a glycol leak. The crew quickly transferred to the spare aircraft ED825 but still took off half an hour late. When they arrived over the Sorpe they were surprised to see no other aircraft from their wave in the area at all. Little did they know that all of them had either been shot down or had been forced to return to base damaged.

Because the Sorpe was an earth built dam with a concrete core, the Upkeep didn't need to bounce across the water, it just had to be laid in the centre from as low as possible. As such the plan was to fly along the length of the dam with the port wing over the crest, and drop the Upkeep roughly half way across.

Between them, pilot Joe McCarthy and bomb aimer 'Johnny' Johnson, took nine attempts to drop in the right place, causing 'Johnny' in his own words to 'rapidly become the most unpopular member of the crew!'

I painted this picture to coincide with us filming the TV documentary about 'Johnny' Johnson and the search for the remains of his Lancaster ED825, the story of which you can read about earlier in this book. The significant landmark in this scene is the church on top of the hill. Johnny explained that Joe McCarthy used this feature to predict where the dam would be as he approached from the other side of the high ground. They came pretty close to the church on a number of the runs but in the end it guided them accurately onto the dam and helped them deliver their Upkeep spot on target.

THE AMERICAN DAMBUSTER
Acrylic on linen, 48" x 20", 2007
Private Collection, New Zealand

Mark Postlethwaite GAvA 01

F-86 Sabre Aces

Major Ed Heller, a WWII Mustang Ace shoots down a MiG-15 over North Korea on 17th November 1952. Flying in his personal F-86 'Hell-er Bust X' he and his wingman spotted two MiG-15s at 35,000ft whilst patrolling 'MiG Alley'. After a short engagement, Heller's MiG went down in flames, his first victory since the end of WWII.

F-86 SABRE ACES
Acrylic on board, 15" x 11", 2005
In the collection of Neil T Bremer

Skyhawk over Vietnam

Lieutenant Dennis J Sapp of VA-55 destroys a SAM missile site on an Iron Hand mission near Haiphong, North Vietnam on 23rd May 1972. Sapp received a DFC for this mission.

SKYHAWK OVER VIETNAM
Acrylic on board, 15" x 11", 2007
Private Collection

F-4 Phantom II

Colonel Robin Olds flying an F-4C Phantom II of the 8th TFW shoots down a MiG 17 on 20th May 1967 over Vietnam. In the Colonel's own words;
'The MiG pilot had three choices. He could bale out, hit that ridge of hills or pull up, giving my Sidewinder a clean shot. He chose the last option'.

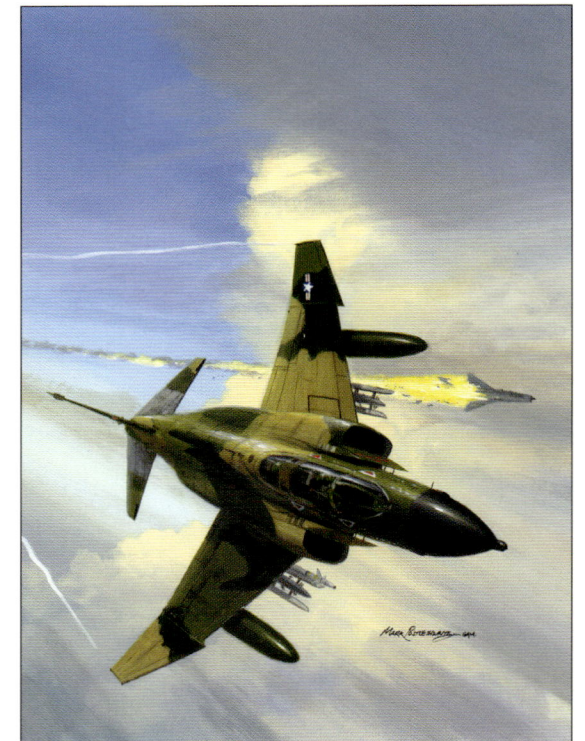

MIG KILLERS
Acrylic on board, 15" x 11", 2005
Private Collection

F-4 PHANTOM II
Acrylic on board, 15" x 11", 2005
In the collection of John Hallberg

F-15E Strike Eagle Units

In the early 2000s four American airmen recorded the longest ever fighter combat sortie timed at 15.5hrs in their F-15E Strike Eagles. The mission over Afghanistan was to attack Taliban Command and Control facilities and involved spending 9 hours loitering over the target area. This painting records the moment when one of the F-15s released four of its nine 500lb Laser Guided bombs.

F-16s OVER BAGHDAD
Acrylic on board, 15" x 11", 2007
In the collection of Phil Needham

F-15E STRIKE EAGLE UNITS
Acrylic on board, 15" x 11", 2007
Private Collection

Moss Intercept

The first intercept of a Tupolev Tu-126 Moss carried out by Norwegian Starfighters on 6th June 1968.

Whilst doing the research for this painting I spoke to one of the Starfighter pilots Erik Dalen. He told me that this interception was totally unexpected and nobody would believe them until they had the photos developed and printed showing indeed that they had just intercepted this rare new Soviet aircraft.

MOSS INTERCEPT
Acrylic on canvas, 42" x 28", 2006
In the collection of the Norwegian Armed Forces

F-16s in the Fjords

F-16s of the RNoAF jink through the coastal fjords on a routine training sortie, present day.

With this painting I just wanted to capture the sheer exhilaration of flying a fast jet at low level through the fjords. I added the man in the boat up ahead just to provide a bit of a story. He'll either really enjoy the next few moments or will use the entire set of Norwegian swear words, depending on his view of low flying aircraft, and if he's caught any fish yet!

F-16s IN THE FJORDS
Acrylic on canvas, 42" x 28", 2009
In the collection of the Norwegian Armed Forces

Acknowledgements

Being an aviation artist is a pretty solitary occupation but nevertheless there are many people who have helped me over the years to make my hobby a career. First of all I should of course mention my wife Asia who finds words of encouragement even though I know she is 'bemused' by most of the things I paint! Then my children Kasia and Szymek who have to put up with Daddy working for seemingly 24 hours a day, every day. Thanks to my brother Mick for running the office in the UK whilst I've been out enjoying the sun and good food in Poland and to my accountant and friend Trevor Wright who has been on this journey with me right from the start and has provided much needed guidance and encouragement over the years.

Thanks to Richard Barratt at Spectrum for a great service and friendship over the years and to Amy Shore (my basement girl) for always trying so hard to make the scans of my paintings look good, no matter how bad the original looks!

Then there are the friends who have over the years provided inspiration and support to enable me to do what I do;

Robert and Agnieszka Lewandowski	*Frida Saracchi*	*Chris and Pam Johnson*
Tomek and Asia Waszkiewicz	*Hallvard and Reidun Vinje*	*Steve and Steph Rawlinson*
Wacław and Danuta Śliwa	*Lyder Amundsen*	*Dennis Oldridge*
Grzesiek Śiwa	*Wing Commander Tom and Eileen Neil*	*Keith Platt*
Paweł and Iza Bagiński	*Paul Wharmby and Kerry Vaughan*	*Simon Parry*
Kasia Gołębiowska	*Brian and Jan Fernley*	*Wesley Cornell*
	Mike and Sandra Seymour	

Thanks to all the Osprey authors who have supplied me the detailed references over the years for their cover paintings, their research provides the details for some of the captions in this book.

And lastly to all of the collectors whose names you'll see next to the paintings in this book. Without them, I'd have to get a proper job, and for that fact alone I offer them all my deepest and heartfelt thanks!

This book is dedicated to my mother Joyce who encouraged me at the beginning, supported me through the hard times and is still there for me whenever I need her.

x